AF132998

Exam FFM
Foundations in Financial Management

Pocket Notes

KAPLAN

PUBLISHING

British library cataloguing-in-publication data

A catalogue record for this book is available from the British Library.

Published by:
Kaplan Publishing UK
Unit 2 The Business Centre
Molly Millars Lane
Wokingham
Berkshire
RG41 2QZ

ISBN 978-1-78740-428-1

© Kaplan Financial Limited, 2019

Printed and bound in Great Britain.

The text in this material and any others made available by any Kaplan Group company does not amount to advice on a particular matter and should not be taken as such. No reliance should be placed on the content as the basis for any investment or other decision or in connection with any advice given to third parties. Please consult your appropriate professional adviser as necessary. Kaplan Publishing Limited and all other Kaplan group companies expressly disclaim all liability to any person in respect of any losses or other claims, whether direct, indirect, incidental, consequential or otherwise arising in relation to the use of such materials.

Contents

Preface

These Pocket Notes contain everything you need to know for the exam, presented in a unique visual way that makes revision easy and effective.

Written by experienced lecturers and authors, these Pocket Notes break down content into manageable chunks to maximise your concentration.

Quality and accuracy are of the utmost importance to us so if you spot an error in any of our products, please send an email to mykaplanreporting@kaplan.com with full details, or follow the link to the feedback form in MyKaplan.

Our Quality Co-ordinator will work with our technical team to verify the error and take action to ensure it is corrected in future editions.

Introduction

In this chapter

- Overview of the assessment.
- Keys to success.

Overview of the assessment

	No. of marks
Section A: 10 MCQs	20
Section B: 6 WTQs	
(10, 15 or 20 marks each)	80
	100

The exam is a two hour paper.

Keys to success

- Ensure you are familiar with the entire syllabus, as this will be examined.

- Practise lots of past examination questions.

- Set out your answers clearly – and don't jump between questions in the examination itself as this may confuse the examiner.

1

Cash and cash flows

In this chapter

- Cash and cash flows.
- Sources and applications of finance.
- Cash flow and profit.
- Cash and accruals accounting.

Cash and cash flows

Definition

Cash: Paper money and money in bank accounts.

Cash flow: Receipts and payments of cash.

Net cash flow: Difference between cash received and cash paid.

Cash inflows vary depending on business type e.g.:

Supermarket	Regular cash inflow
Hats	Seasonal – spring and summer
Ice cream	Seasonal – summer
College	Irregular – whenever courses start

Cash cycle and operating cycle

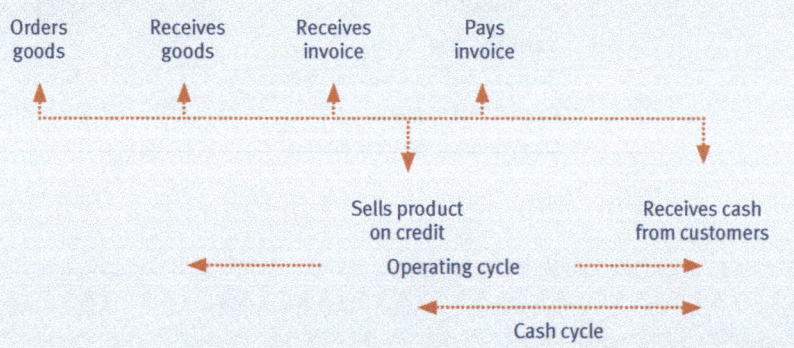

Sources and applications of finance

Sources of cash	Uses of cash
Obtaining finance: • Increase in long-term debt • Increase in equity • Increase in current liabilities Selling assets • Decrease in current assets • Decrease in non-current assets	Paying payables or stockholders: • Decrease in long-term debt • Decrease in equity • Decrease in current liabilities Buying assets • Increase in current assets • Increase in non-current assets

Receipts	Payments
Revenue	
• Cash sales • Payments by receivables	• Trade payables (goods and services purchased) • Employees (salaries) • Sundry expenses (petty cash)
Capital	
• Money from shareholders/capital from owners • Non-current asset sales	• Non-current asset purchases
Drawings / dividends	
	• Drawings (sole trader / partnership) • Dividends (limited company)
Exceptional (unplanned)	
• Items not mentioned above	• Items not mentioned above

Cash flow and profit

- Profit = excess of income over expenditure in statement of profit or loss.
- For business to survive, cash inflows must exceed cash outflows.
- Cash flow and profits are different.
- Business can make a profit, but still have negative cash flows.

Reasons for differences in cash flows and profits

Business activity	Effect on cash and profit
Purchase of non-current asset	Cash outflow, no effect on profit
Depreciation charge on statement of profit or loss	No effect on cash, profit decreased
Increase in working capital (e.g. inventory purchase)	Cash outflow, no effect on profit
Normal trading	See below

Statement of profit or loss		Cash effect		
	January	January	February	March
	$	$	$	$
Sale	1,000		1,000	
Purchase	(600)			(600)
Gross profit	400			
Wages	(200)	(200)		
Light and heat	(100)		(100)	
Net profit	100			
Cumulative cash flow		(200)	700	100

From January sales only:

- Sales made in January give profit in January.
- Cash flow in January is negative because employees must be paid; no cash received.
- Cash flow in February is positive because receivables have now been paid.
- Only in March does cash flow = profit when payables finally paid.

Definition

Liquidity: Cash or items that can be converted into cash quickly.

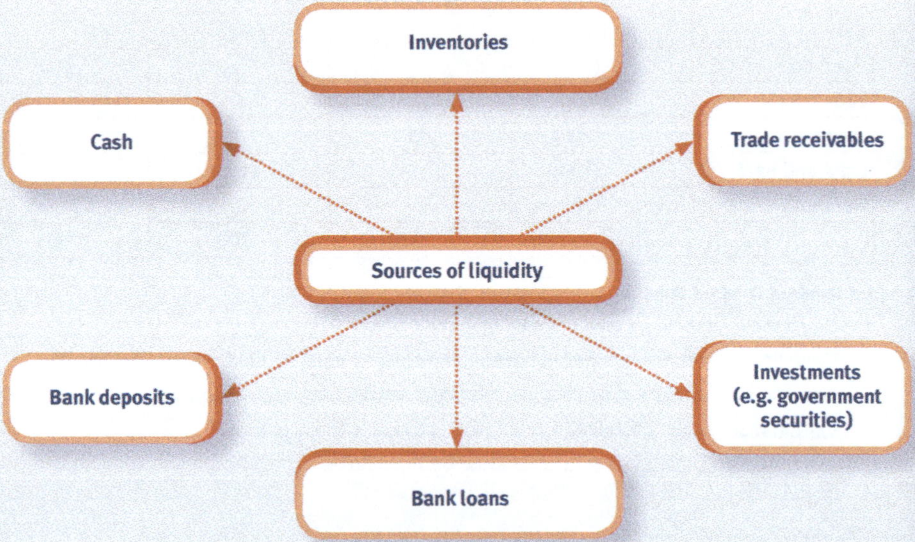
Inventories
Cash
Trade receivables
Sources of liquidity
Bank deposits
Investments (e.g. government securities)
Bank loans

Cash and accruals accounting

Definition

Cash management: Systems and procedures for controlling cash flows and the use of cash in a business.

Cash accounting: Recording income when received and expenditure when it is incurred.

Accruals accounting: Recording income and expenditure when earned.

Different accounting methods give different results.

In previous cash flow example. In January:

- Cash accounting = cash outflow of $200
- Accurals accounting = profit of $100.

Exam focus

Ensure you understand the difference between profit and cash flows and the difference between accruals and cash accounting.

2

Cash budgets

In this chapter

- Objectives and types of cash budget.
- Format of a cash budget.
- Preparing a receipts and payments budget.
- Statement of financial position forecast.
- Sensitivity analysis.
- Forecasting with inflation.
- Cleared funds.
- Monitoring cash flows.

Objectives and types of cash budget

Cash budget: A detailed forecast of cash inflows and outflows for a future time period, incorporating revenue and capital items and other cash flow items.

| Types of | Cash budgets | Objectives of |

Receipts and payments. Forecast receipts and payments based on predicted sales and purchases

Anticipate cash shortage/surplus and make plans for dealing with these

Statement of financial position forecast. Forecast future statement of financial position based on past statement of financial position. Cash derived as balancing figure

Provide basis against which actual cash flow can be monitored

Budgeting a cash deficit

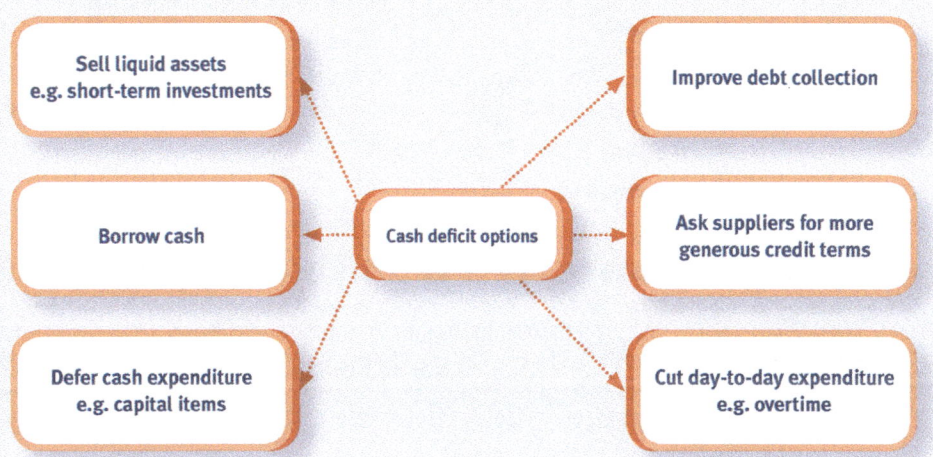

Format of a cash budget

Cash receipts (itemised)

−

Cash payments (itemised)

=

Net cash flow for month

+

Cash balance b/f from last month

=

Cash balance c/f to next month

 Prepared for each month

Cash budget normally prepared from forecast statement of profit or loss.

Shows how cash receipts and payments align with statement of profit or loss entries.

Cash items normally lag behind statement of profit or loss.

Preparing a receipts and payments budget

1. Calculate receipts from sales

1. Calculate actual sales per month.
2. Estimate % of cash sales.
3. Estimate months in which credit sales will pay.
4. Calculate cash receipts each month.

Sales in			Jan	Feb	March	April
Jan	50,000					
	5%	Cash ·············▶	2,500			
	50%	Received in 1 month ·············▶		25,000		
	45%	Received in 2 months ······································▶			22,500	
Feb	75,000					
	5%	Cash ···································▶		3,750		
	50%	Received in 1 month ·····································▶			37,500	
	45%	Received in 2 months ··▶				33,750
Cash received			**2,500**	**28,750**	**60,000**	**33,750**

2. Determine purchases of materials

1. Calculate raw materials required.
2. Find number of items to sell from sales budget.
3. Calculate units of raw material (assume here 4 for each item produced).
4. Allow for inventory building (5,000 more items needed in Feb).
5. Calculate total units each month.
6. Value at unit price (assumed $0.50 each).

Units produced and sold			Jan	Feb
Jan				
	10,000 produced	Units needed ┈┈┈┈┈┈┈►	40,000	
Feb				
	15,000 produced	Units needed ┈┈┈┈┈┈┈┈┈┈┈►		60,000
	5,000 for inventory	Units needed ┈┈┈┈┈┈┈┈┈┈┈►		20,000
Units needed			40,000	80,000
			@50c each	
Purchase price			**20,000**	**40,000**

3. Calculate payments to suppliers

1. Find purchase amounts (from above section).
2. Determine when suppliers will be paid (assume after delay of 1 or 2 months here).
3. Calculate payments made for each month's purchases.
4. Calculate total cash payments to suppliers.

Purchased in			Jan	Feb	March	April
Jan	20,000					
	60%	Paid in 1 month ·······················▶		12,000		
	40%	Paid in 2 months ··▶			8,000	
Feb	40,000					
	60%	Paid in 1 month ···▶			24,000	
	40%	Paid in 2 months ···▶				16,000
Cash payments			0	12,000	32,000	16,000

4. Calculate other payments

1. Calculate variable overheads based on production. Assume $1 per unit produced.

2. Enter any fixed costs in the correct months.

Variable overheads			Jan	Feb	March	April
At $1 per item produced						
Jan	10,000	Paid in 1 month ················▶		10,000		
Feb	20,000	Paid in 1 months ··▶			20,000	
Fixed costs						
Salaries	Paid each month ··············▶		5,000	5,000	5,000	5,000
Cash payments			5,000	15,000	25,000	5,000

5. **Prepare total cash flow**

   1. Take cash receipts.

   2. Deduct purchases and other payments.

   3. Add cash balance b/f.

   4. Calculate cash balance c/f.

   5. Remember c/f cash balance is the b/f in the next month.

	Jane	Feb	March	April
Cash receipts	2,500	28,750	60,000	33,750
−				
Cash payments – purchases	0	12,000	32,000	16,000
−				
Cash payments – other	5,000	15,000	25,000	5,000
=				
Net cash flow for month	-2,500	1,750	3,000	12,750
+				
Cash balance b/f	5,000	2,500	4,250	7,250
=				
Cash balance c/f	**2,500**	**4,250**	**7,250**	**20,000**

Note: This example only uses sales and purchases in January and February – in practice a cash flow forecast is based on sales and purchases for all months of the year.

Other receipts and payments are entered into the forecast as required e.g. capital purchases, taxation payments, dividend payments.

Statement of financial position forecast

Definition

Statement of financial position based forecast: An estimate of an enterprise's statement of financial position at a future date. It is used to identify cash shortfall/surplus.

1. Calculate changes in all statement of financial position figures.
2. Find cash figure as the 'balancing' figure on the statement of financial position.

Exam focus

The basic principles of cash budgeting were shown in this chapter. Examination questions may require you to prepare a cash budget, so ensure you understand the differences between transactions occurring and the cash movement for those transactions.

Sensitivity analysis

Sensitivity analysis: A modelling and risk assessment procedure in which changes are made to significant variables in order to see how changes will affect planned outcome.

Sensitivity analysis is commonly performed on the following items:

- Sales.
- Cost of goods sold/gross profit.
- Operating expenses.
- Interest rates.
- Receivables collection period.
- Inventory stockholding days.
- Payables payment period.
- Non-current asset purchases/reductions.

Sensitivity analysis – strengths and weaknesses

Strengths	Weaknesses
<ul><li>No complicated theory to understand.</li><li>Information presented to management in a form that facilitates subjective judgement to decide the likelihood of the various possible outcomes considered.</li></ul>	<ul><li>It assumes that changes to variables can be made independently, e.g. material prices will change independently of other variables.</li><li>It only identifies how far a variable needs to change; it does not look at the probability of such a change.</li><li>It only provides information on the basis of which decisions can be made. It does not point to the correct decision directly.</li></ul>

Forecasting with inflation

Inflation: The process whereby the price of commodities steadily rises over time.

Index number: Shows the rate of change of a variable from one specified time to another.

Simple price index = $\dfrac{p_1}{p_0}$ x 100

Where:

p_0 is the price at time 0

p_1 is the price at time 1

Simple quantity index = $\dfrac{q_1}{q_0}$ x 100

Where:

q_0 is the quantity at time 0

q_1 is the quantity at time 1

Weighting the index

- By using appropriate weights, price relatives can be combined to give a multi-item price index.

- To determine the weighting, we need information about the relative importance of each item.

- A weighted index can be calculated using the following formula:

Weighted index = $\dfrac{\sum qp_1}{\sum qp_0}$ x 100

Cleared funds

Definition

Cleared funds: Amounts sent from payee to recipient actually in recipient's bank account and available for making payments.

- Bank account balance does not always show cleared funds.
- Non-cash deposits take up to three days to clear.

Exam focus

Ensure you can explain changes in cash budgets, not simply prepare them.

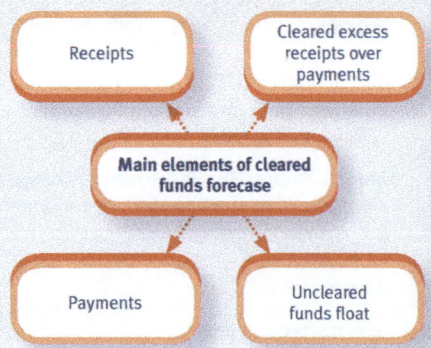

Receipts

Cleared excess receipts over payments

Main elements of cleared funds forecase

Payments

Uncleared funds float

Monitoring cash flows

Definition

Cash flow report: Compares budgeted to actual cash flow.

Items to check when monitoring actual cash flows:

Cash receipts	Cash payments
• Volume of sales meets budget. • Receivables collections on time.	• Routine payments (e.g. rent and salaries) made on time. • Payments relating to activity level (e.g. purchases, wages) follow the activity level. • Non-recurring payments (e.g. taxation, dividends) paid on time.

If actual receipts and payments indicate budget incorrect, then amend cash budget.

3

Cash management

In this chapter

- Managing cash balances.
- Cash management models.
- Treasury management.
- Procedures, authorisation and security.

Managing cash balances

Definition

Cash management: Practices and techniques designed to:

- Accelerate and control collections.
- Ensure prompt deposit of receipts.
- Ensure control over payment methods.
- Eliminate idle cash balances.

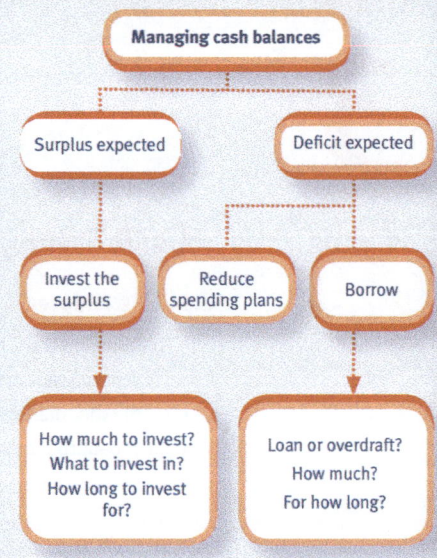

Cash management models

The role of the cash manager is to monitor and control exposure risks.

```
┌─────────────────────┐     ┌─────────────────────┐
│ Risk that cash      │     │ Risk that if faced  │
│ receipts < expected │     │ with cash shortage  │
│                     │     │ business cannot     │
│                     │     │ raise cash needed   │
└─────────────────────┘     └─────────────────────┘

        ┌─────────────────────────┐
        │ Cash flows and liquidity │
        └─────────────────────────┘

┌─────────────────────┐     ┌─────────────────────┐
│ Risk that cash      │     │ Risk of investing   │
│ receipts > expected │     │ surplus cash and    │
│                     │     │ earning less        │
│                     │     │ interest/losing     │
│                     │     │ deposits through    │
│                     │     │ bank failure        │
└─────────────────────┘     └─────────────────────┘
```

Definition

Liquidity: Means having cash or ready access to funds. A business cannot operate if it is unable to pay its bills, so sufficient cash/other short-term assets must be readily available.

Levels of liquidity

Levels of liquidity increase from left to right. Cash is the most liquid asset.

Non-current assets → Inventory → Receivables → Short-term investments → Cash at bank and in hand

Baumol's model

The Baumol model assumes the cash manager invests excess funds in interest-bearing securities and liquidates them to meet the firm's demand for cash.

- If cash resources steadily used up by constant daily demand can apply Baumol's model.
- This model calculates optimum regular cash injection to current account (x).
- Formula for Baumol's model shown below:

$$x = \sqrt{\frac{2 \times \text{Annual cash disbursements} \times \text{Cost per sale of securities}}{\text{Interest rate}}}$$

Limitations of Baumol's model:

- Does not allow cash flows to fluctuate.
- In practice, firms do not use constant daily amounts of cash.
- Firms are not able to predict daily cash inflows and outflows.

Exam focus

The Baumol model formula is not examinable, but you may have to explain how the model works.

Treasury management

Treasury management: Covers activities concerned with managing the liquidity of a business – essential for the survival and growth of a business.

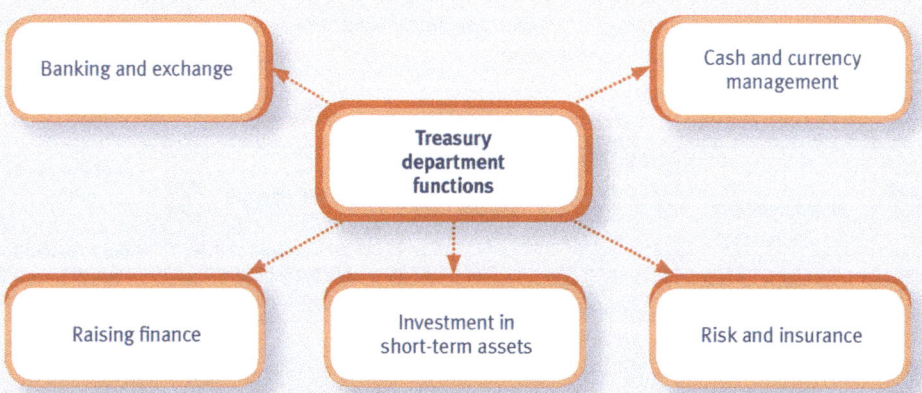

Procedures, authorisation and security

- Cash management is a day-to-day concern.
- Decisions must be taken quickly about investing and cashing in investments.
- One of the most important procedures in cash management is 'cash handling'.

Cash handling procedures

Accountability
Requires that person carrying out task has the authority to do so

Reconciliation
Requires assurance that transactions are properly documented and approved and verifies processing and recording of transactions

Physical security
Assurance that the safety of people and assets (specifically cash) is maintained and controlled

Segragation of duties
Ensures that no one is put in a position in which they are able to commit and conceal an error or fraud

4

Investing surplus funds

In this chapter

- Surplus funds.
- Investing cash surpluses.
- Types of investment.
- Marketable securities.
- Capital market instruments.

Surplus funds

Definition

Surplus funds: Comprise liquid balances not needed to finance current business operations and not held permanently for short-term investments.

- Long-term surpluses: cash surpluses that a business has no forseeable use for (rare).
- Short-term surpluses: need to be invested temporarily until required.

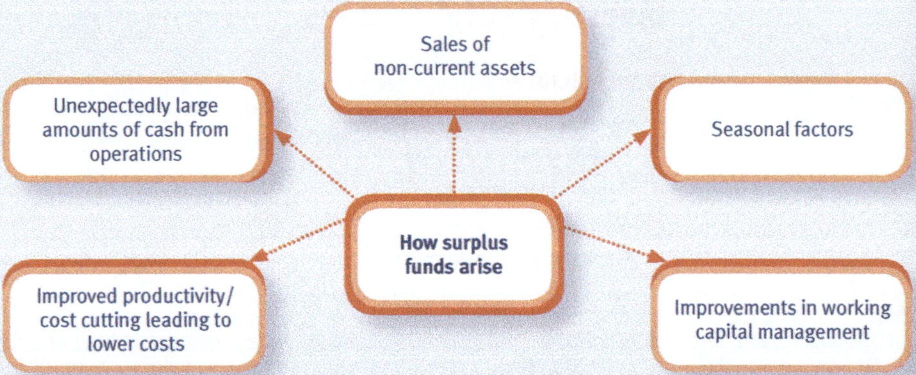

Sales of non-current assets

Unexpectedly large amounts of cash from operations

Seasonal factors

How surplus funds arise

Improved productivity/ cost cutting leading to lower costs

Improvements in working capital management

Investing cash surpluses

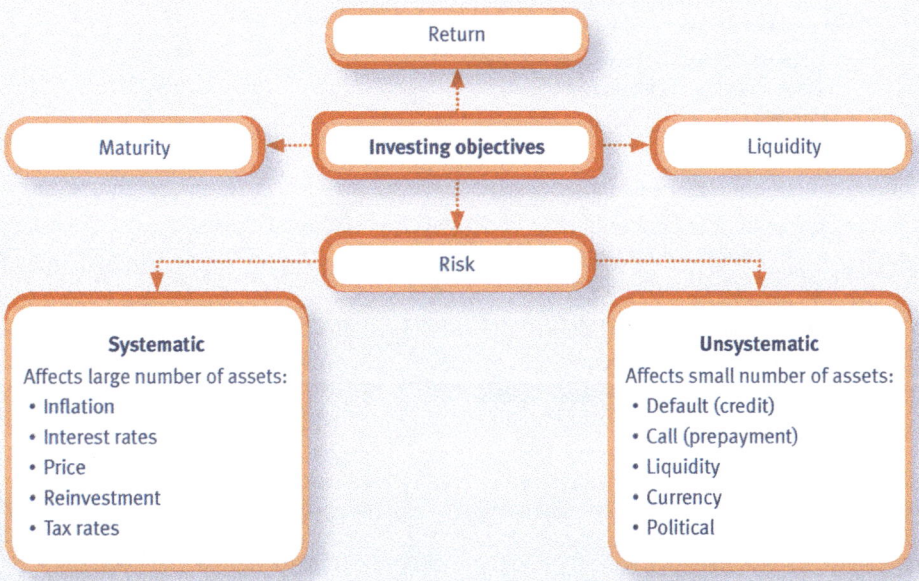

Exposure to investment risk

- Lower risk investments include deposit accounts with reputable banks.
- Higher risk investments include money market investments and government securities.

Short-term investments

- Aim: Obtain higher return than holding cash.
- Funds available quickly (liquid).
- Minimise risk of capital losing value.

Long-term investments

- Aim: Provide long-run return.
- Liquidity n/a – funds not needed quickly.
- Minimise investment risk.

Types of investment

A wide number of short-term investment opportunities are available – each offering various degrees of liquidity, risk and return.

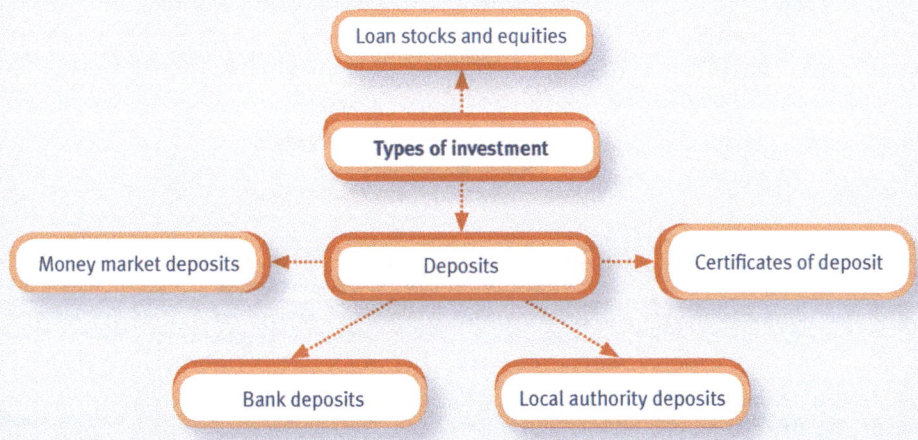

Marketable securities

Marketable securities: Stocks and bonds that can be traded between investors – they have a readily determined fair market value and can be converted into cash at any time.

```
Indirect investments  ◄┄┄┄  Marketable securities  ┄┄┄►  Capital market securities
                                      │
                                      ▼
                            Money Market Securities
```

CDs	Gilts	Bills of Exchange	Treasury bills
Certificate of deposit: financial instrument issued by bank certifying holder to right of fixed-term deposit of funds at specified interest rate.	Gilt-edged securities: marketable British Government secuities. Usually have fixed interest rates, categorised according to redemption dates (shor-, medium-, long-dated) Some gilts are index-linked	An unconditional order in writing from one person to another, requiring person to whom it is written to pay a specified sum of money. Sight bill = payable immediately. Term bill = payable at specified future date	Short-term debt instruments issued and sold by central government. Usually have term of 91 days when issued. Can be described as a 'You Owe Me'

Bills of exchange – trade bill

Drawer Supplier goods	2 Sends bill to drawee	**Drawee** Customer for goods
1 Prepares bill	·····▶	
5 Either waits for payment date and presents to bank for payment or sells bill (e.g. to bank) at discount to obtain money before payment date	4 Bill returned to drawer	3 Signs bill – 'accepts' bill, confirms will pay on due date

Risky because drawee may not pay on maturity of bill.

Discounting bank bills

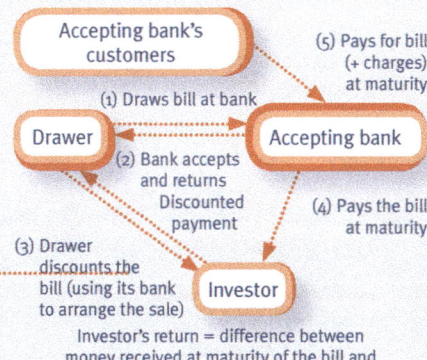

Accepting bank's customers

(5) Pays for bill (+ charges) at maturity

(1) Draws bill at bank

Drawer

Accepting bank

(2) Bank accepts and returns Discounted payment

(4) Pays the bill at maturity

(3) Drawer discounts the bill (using its bank to arrange the sale)

Investor

Investor's return = difference between money received at maturity of the bill and the discounted amount paid for the bill.

The discount market

A business with short-term cash surpluses can arrange to invest in the discount market.

Interest rate risk

- Zero if investor holds bills to maturity.
- Only exists for investors who intend to buy and then re-sell before maturity.

- If market rates of interest ↑, market value of bills ↓
- If market rates of interest ↓, market value of bills ↑

Capital market instruments

Share capital:

- A security that represents a portion of the owner's capital in a business.
- Ordinary share = equity share = risk capital of a company.
- Preferred share – comparable to loan notes.
- Various types of preferred share:
  - Participating
  - Cumulative
  - Non-cumulative
  - Redeemable
  - Convertible.

Fixed income securities

Loan notes:

- Similar to a mortgage.
- Long-term loan secured on certain fixed or floating assets of a company.

Loan stocks:

- Security issued by company in respect of a loan made by investors.
- Can be secured, unsecured, convertible or non-convertible.

5

Working capital management

In this chapter

- Working capital management.
- Liquidity ratios.
- Working capital ratios.
- Working capital management and solvency.

Working capital management

Working capital cycle: Average length of time between paying for purchases of materials and receiving payment from receivables after a sale has been made.

Elements of cycle:

Average inventory turnover period:
Average time from buying inventory to using in a sale

+

Average receivables collection period (debtor days):
Average time from making sale to receiving payment from customer

–

Average period of credit taken from trade payables (creditor days):
Average number of days taken to pay suppliers

=

Working capital cycle

Liquidity ratios

Current ratio: Ratio of current assets to current liabilities.

Acid test ratio: Ratio of liquid assets (i.e. current assets excluding inventory) to the current liabilities.

Ratio	Calculation	Meaning
Current ratio	$$\frac{\text{Current assets}}{\text{Current liabilities}}$$	>1 good – business has more assets than liabilities – can pay debts as fall due. <1 bad as cannot pay all current liabilities from current assets.
Quick or acid ratio	$$\frac{\text{Current assets excluding inventory}}{\text{Current liabilities}}$$	>1 good – business can pay liabilities from cash and collections from debtors. <1 normally bad as business lacks cash to pay liabilities.

Working capital ratios

Ratio	Calculation	Meaning
Inventory turnover period	$\dfrac{\text{Average inventory}}{\text{Annual cost of sales}} \times 365 \text{ days}$	The higher the ratio, the more time is taken to turn inventory into sales.
Receivables collection period	$\dfrac{\text{Average receivables}}{\text{Sales}} \times 365 \text{ days}$	The higher the ratio the more time is being taken for customers to pay their debts.
Payables payment period	$\dfrac{\text{Average payables}}{\text{Cost of sales}} \times 365 \text{ days}$	The higher the ratio the more time the company is taking to pay suppliers.

Exam focus

Ensure that you can remember the calculation of the different ratios in this section as you may need to perform these in the exam.

Monitoring the working capital cycle

Working capital turnover period	Days
Average inventory turnover	81
Average credit to customers	45
	126
Average credit from suppliers	89
Average working capital cycle	**37**

KAPLAN PUBLISHING

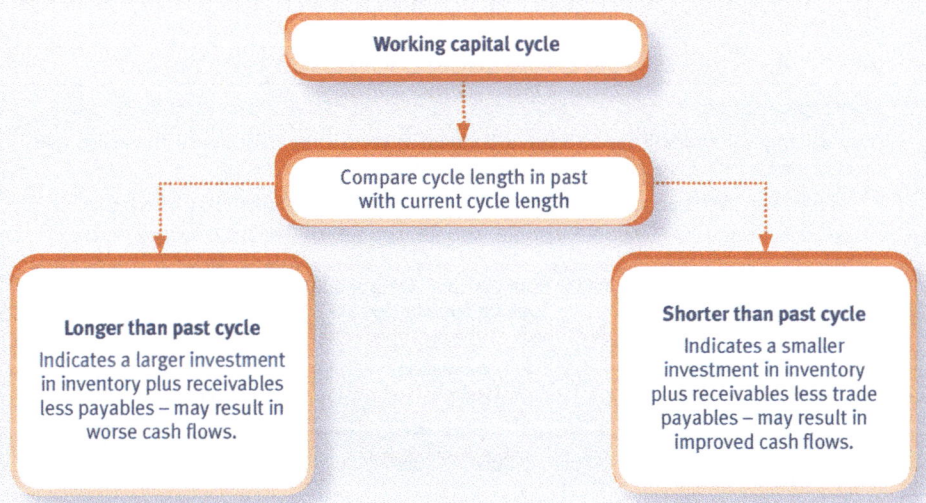

Working capital cycle

Compare cycle length in past with current cycle length

Longer than past cycle

Indicates a larger investment in inventory plus receivables less payables – may result in worse cash flows.

Shorter than past cycle

Indicates a smaller investment in inventory plus receivables less trade payables – may result in improved cash flows.

Working capital management and solvency

Definition

Overcapitalisation: A firm is overcapitalised if its working capital is excessive for its needs.

Overtrading: Overtrading occurs when a business is conducting its business operations with inadequate capital. It is also called undercapitalisation.

- Ratios and cash budgets used to monitor cash flows and liquidity.

- Cash shortage may be indicative of overtrading.

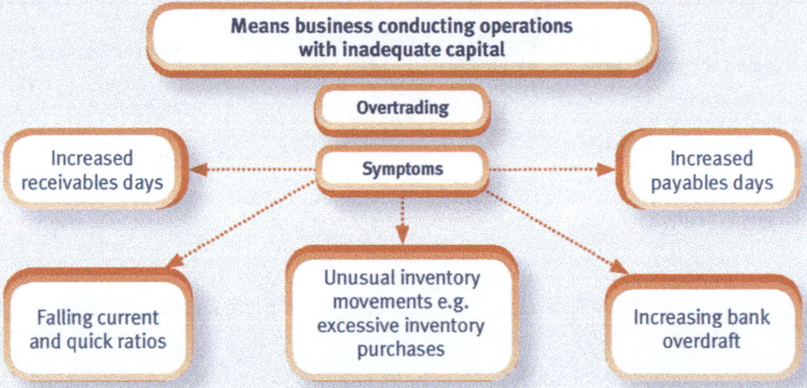

```
                    Means business conducting operations
                         with inadequate capital

                              Overtrading

  Increased                    Symptoms                    Increased
  receivables days                                         payables days

  Falling current         Unusual inventory            Increasing bank
  and quick ratios        movements e.g.               overdraft
                          excessive inventory
                          purchases
```

chapter

6

Working capital management: inventory and payables

In this chapter

- Management of inventory.
- EOQ and its application.
- Discounts and the EOQ.
- JIT and lean manufacturing.
- Management of trade payables.
- Payables control operations.
- Supplier payment methods.

Management of inventory

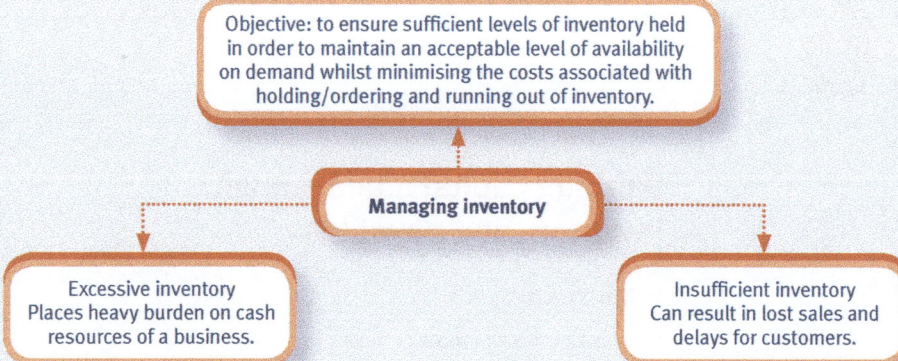

Objective: to ensure sufficient levels of inventory held in order to maintain an acceptable level of availability on demand whilst minimising the costs associated with holding/ordering and running out of inventory.

Managing inventory

Excessive inventory
Places heavy burden on cash resources of a business.

Insufficient inventory
Can result in lost sales and delays for customers.

Ratio	Calculation	Meaning
Inventory turnover ratio	$\dfrac{\text{Cost of sales}}{\text{Average inventory held}}$	Number of times average inventory has been sold during the year.

Manufacturing companies split ratio into raw materials, work-in-progress and finished goods to show effect on different sections of inventory.

Costs of inventory

Lead time: Time from start of process until process completion.

Stockout: Costs of running out of inventory.

Buffer inventory: 'Excess' inventory held to protect against interruptions in supply. Also called safety inventory.

Re-order quantity: Number of units of inventory in one order.

Re-order level: Level of inventory at which a replenishment order should be placed.

Economic Order Quantity: Economic inventory replenishment size – minimises the ordering and holding costs.

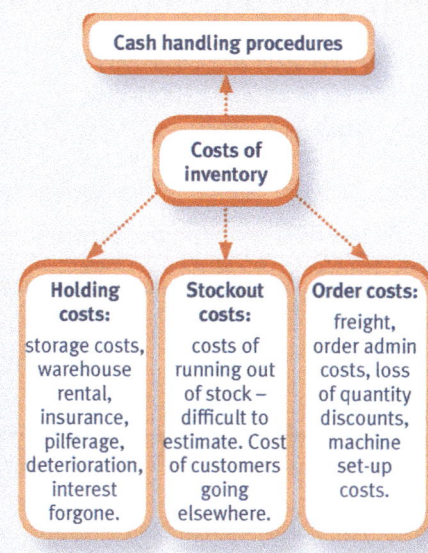

EOQ and its application

Key questions about inventory:

- How much inventory to order?
- When to re-order?

Aim to:

- Limit investment in inventory, but
- To ensure stockouts do not occur.

APPLY EOQ

Ordering more frequently	Ordering less frequently
Higher ordering costs	Lower ordering costs
Smaller average inventory	Larger average inventory

The EOQ formula calculates the optimal amount of inventory to be re-ordered each time an order is placed.

$$EOQ = \sqrt{\frac{2 \times Co \times D}{Ch}}$$

C_o = Cost of placing one order

D = Expected annual sales volume (demand)

Ch = Annual cost of holding one item in inventory

So if:

CO = $200

D = 30,000

Ch = $1.2

$$EOQ = \sqrt{\frac{2 \times 200 \times 30,000}{1.2}}$$

EOQ therefore = 3,162

This will be rounded to say 3,500 for ease of ordering.

DISCOUNTS MAY AFFECT THE EOQ!

Re-order level: Demand x Lead time

Remember! The EOQ is ordered when the re-order level is reached.

Discounts and the EOQ

A common task in exam questions is to ask students to evaluate whether bulk discounts are worth taking.

Procedure

1   Calculate EOQ with no discount.

2   If EOQ is below discount level, calculate total annual inventory costs.

3   Recalculate annual inventory costs with order size needed to obtain discount.

4   Select minimum cost alternative from steps 2 and 3 above.

5   Repeat for all discount levels.

Example

(using above data: unit price = $12)

2% discount available on orders > 5,000 units

Step 1 EOQ about 3,000
Step 2

Purchase costs (30,000 × $12)	360,000
Holding costs (3,000/12) × $1.20)	1,800
Order costs (30,000/3,000) × $200)	2,000
Total costs	363,800

Step 3 (order quantity of 5,000)

Purchase costs (30,000 × $12)	360,000
Holding costs ((5,000/12) × ($1.20 × .98)	2,940
Order costs ((30,000/5,000) × $200	1,200
Total costs	356,940

Step 4

Original cost	363,800
Revised cost	356,940
Cost saving	6,860

Inventory warning levels

Formulae for establishing maximum and minimum warning levels for an item of inventory are as follows:

Minimum inventory level:

Re-order level – (Maximum rate of usage x Maximum lead time).

Maximum inventory level:

Re-order level + Re-order quantity – (Minimum rate of usage x Minimum lead time).

JIT and lean manufacturing

Just-in-time: Procurement of inventory as those items are required by customer rather than hold inventory.

Just-in-time production: Items produced only when needed in the next stage of production.

Just-in-time purchasing: Receipt and usage of raw materials are scheduled, as far as possible, to coincide.

> **Objective of both systems: Items produced only when needed eliminating work-in-progress and finished goods stocks**

Lean manufacturing

Minimal stocks held

Features

JIT production

Limited number of suppliers – who maintain inventory for company

Work on 'pull through' – components drawn into system when needed for final production

Needs good transport links to deliver goods as required

EOQ irrelevant as inventory delivered as needed

Management of trade payables

Trade credit: Company is able to obtain goods from supplier without making immediate payment for those goods.

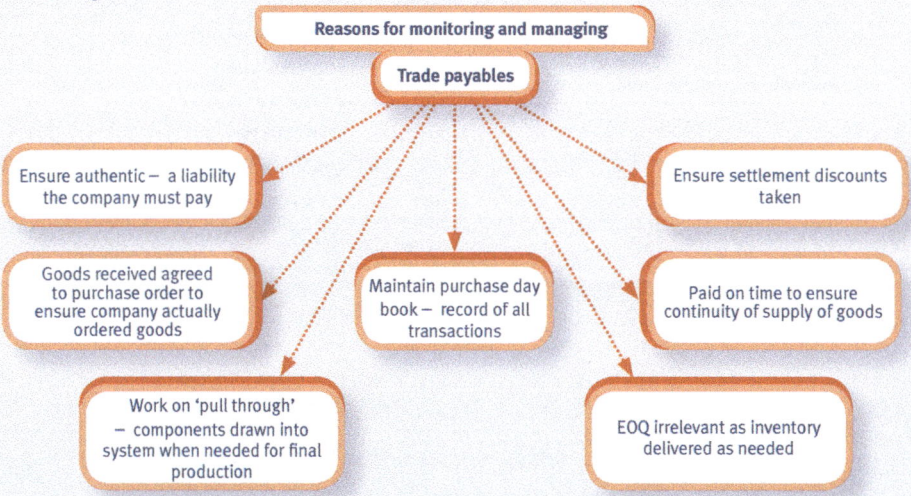

Payables control operations

- Payments should only be made for genuine goods.
- Most payments will have documentary evidence.
- Payments must be authorised.
- Key element of control – suppliers' invoices and statements.

Supplier payment methods

- Cash (through petty cash system).
- Cheque (to pay for invoice).
- Cheque requisition (when there is no invoice).
- Bank giro payments.
- Bankers' Draft.
- Plastic cards.
- Direct Debits.
- Standing Orders.
- CHAPS.
- BACS.
- Telegraphic transfer.

7

Managing receivables

In this chapter

- Giving credit.
- Elements of credit control.
- Credit policy.
- Assessing creditworthiness.
- Credit reference agency reports.
- Financial statement analysis.
- Credit scoring.
- Settlement discounts.
- Rejecting credit applications.
- Legal issues.

Giving credit

Trade credit:

- Given to customers in normal course of business operations.
- Most businesses are forced to give some credit in order to make sales.

Cost of giving credit:

- May generate irrecoverable debts – lose cost of making sale.
- Cost of capital – providing finance to receivables – less cash available for business.

Credit terms:

- Credit limit – total amount of credit allowed.
- Payment date – period of time from invoice date when payment due (30, 60, 90 days?).

Credit and cash flows:

- Giving credit affects cash flows.
- Cash from sales is often most important source of liquidity for a company.

Elements of credit control

Objectives of credit control:

- To achieve balance in giving credit between extra sales/higher irrecoverable debts.
- To limit total amount of trade credit in order to avoid liquidity shortage.

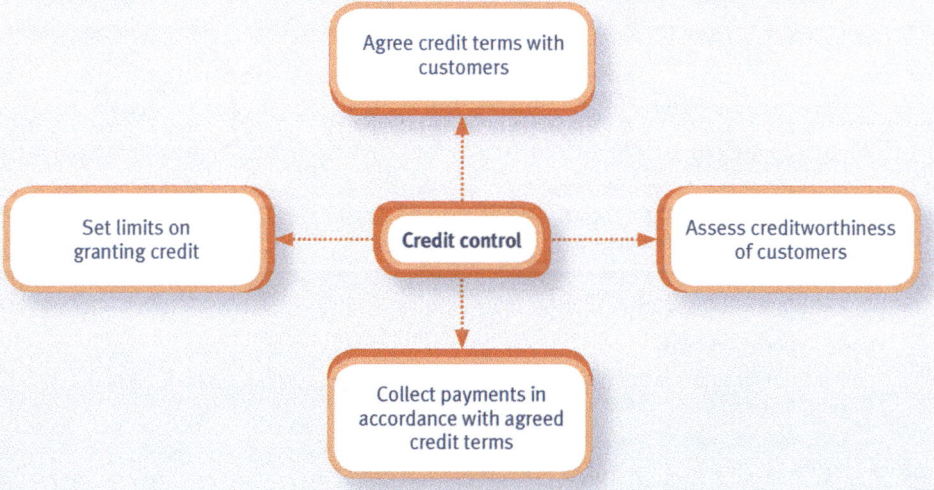

Credit policy

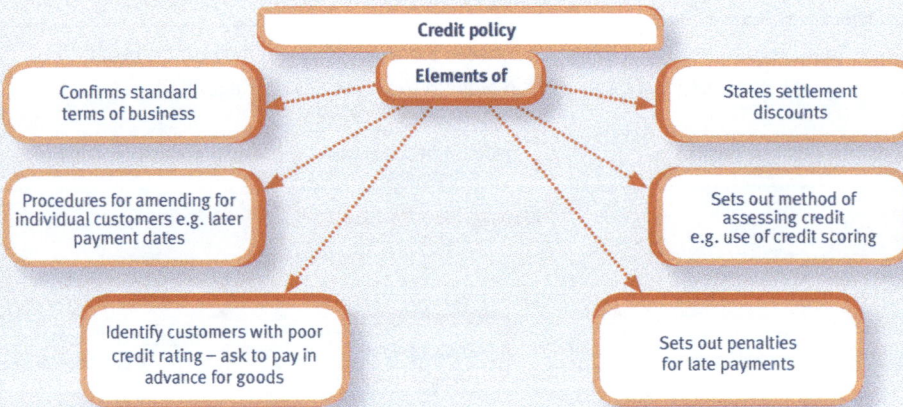

Credit policy

Elements of

Confirms standard terms of business

States settlement discounts

Procedures for amending for individual customers e.g. later payment dates

Sets out method of assessing credit e.g. use of credit scoring

Identify customers with poor credit rating – ask to pay in advance for goods

Sets out penalties for late payments

Credit application form

- Standard form where company or individual applies for credit.
- Customer authorises business to carry out credit checks.

- Use of standard form means credit procedures easier to carry out.

Assessing creditworthiness

Credit status based on:

- Customer's financial health.
- Customer's history of late payments.

Sources – credit status information

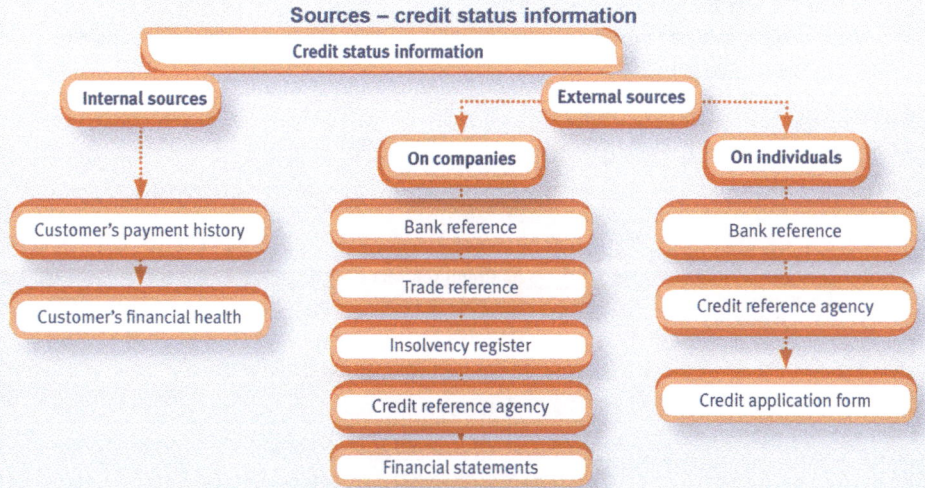

Credit reference agency reports

Credit reference agency reports

- Credit reports on individuals and businesses.
- Can include financial statements and agency's own opinion of creditworthiness.
- Rating given as star value 4 = good to 1 = poor.
- Information obtained from sources similar to those in credit status information diagram.
- Cost about £20 in UK.

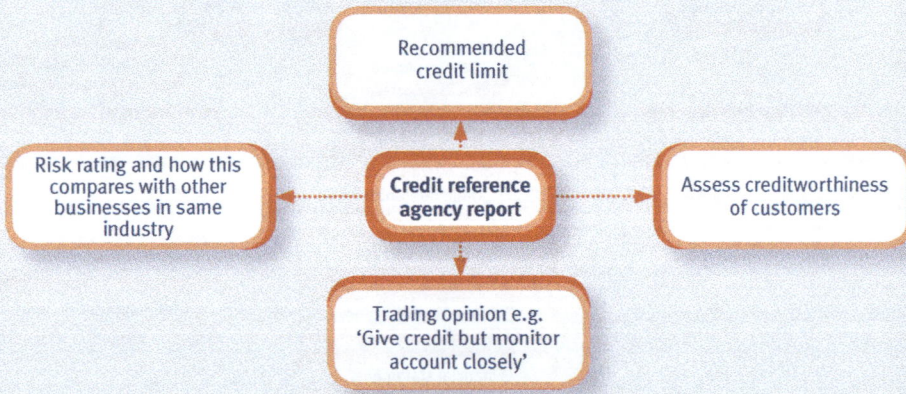

Financial statement analysis

Overview

- Carried out mainly using ratio analysis.
- Other ratios can be used such as interest cover and net profit %.

Weaknesses with ratios

- Show one point in time – can be 'window dressed'.
- Can be approximate measures – not absolute.
- Danger if use in isolation without finding reasons for the ratios.

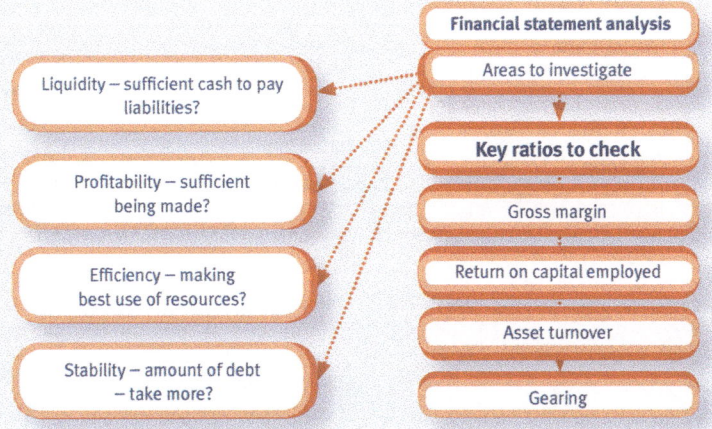

Liquidity – sufficient cash to pay liabilities?

Profitability – sufficient being made?

Efficiency – making best use of resources?

Stability – amount of debt – take more?

Financial statement analysis

Areas to investigate

Key ratios to check

Gross margin

Return on capital employed

Asset turnover

Gearing

Gross margin =	$\dfrac{\text{Gross profit}}{\text{Sales}} \times 100\%$	Profitability checked by comparisons with similar companies.
ROCE =	$\dfrac{\text{Profit before interest and taxation}}{\text{Capital employed}} \times 100\%$	ROCE checked over time to ensure not getting worse and by comparison with similar companies.
Asset turnover =	$\dfrac{\text{Sales}}{\text{Capital employed}}$	Measures sales per \$1 assets employed. Shows efficiency of business. Also use inventory turnover.
Gearing =	$\dfrac{\text{Borrowing}}{\text{Capital employed}} \times 100\%$	Proportion of assets financed by long-term borrowing. Higher ratios = higher risk to business of fall in sales.

Credit scoring

Definition

Credit scoring: Technique allowing companies to apply a systematic approach to the granting of credit – building score of customer's credit.

Credit scoring procedure

1. Number of key items measured

2. Maximum score allocated to each measure

3. Customer scored up to maximum score for each measure

4. Total score derived is indicative of customer's credit status

Example – credit scoring

	Financially strong	Financially stable	Financially weak
Prompt payer	A rating	B rating	E rating
Late payer	C rating	D rating	F rating

Exam focus

When there is a written contract between supplier and customer, it is appropriate to include terms and conditions relating to general credit terms.

Where a written contract covers just one business transaction, the specific credit terms should be included, stating when the customer should pay amounts due.

Settlement discounts

Discount allowed from the invoice payment due if invoice paid within a specific period of time.

Example

Discount of 2% of payment within 14 days of invoice date, net 60 days **means**:

- Payment within 14 days can take 2% discount
- Payments between 15 and 60 days pay invoice amount
- Payments after 60 days may incur credit charge.

Why use settlement discounts?

- Improve cash flow.
- Decrease number of receivables.
- Decrease number of irrecoverable debts by providing an incentive for payment.

Rejecting credit applications

Rejecting credit applications – procedure

1. Notify customer

2. Suggest alternative payment methods

3. Suggest re-apply for credit at later date when more established credit history

Reasons for rejecting credit applications

- Poor credit rating score.
- Poor financial performance.
- New business therefore no track record.
- Customer already has extensive debts.

Legal issues

```
                    ┌─────────────────────┐
              ┌·····│  Refusal to pay debt │·····┐
              ·     └─────────────────────┘     ·
              ▼                                   ▼
     ┌─────────────────┐              ┌─────────────────────┐
     │   Grounds for   │              │ Issues with payment │
     └─────────────────┘              └─────────────────────┘
```

┌────────────────────────────┐   ┌─────────────────────────────┐   ┌───────────────────────────┐
│ Contents of payables ledger │   │ Must be contract – with offer │···▶│ Contract based on written │
│ account   │   │ and acceptance e.g. customer │   │ terms and conditions   │
└────────────────────────────┘   │ offers to purchase goods   │   └───────────────────────────┘
                                     │ and supplier agrees to   │
                                     │ provide those goods   │
┌────────────────────────────┐   └─────────────────────────────┘   ┌───────────────────────────┐
│ Supplier in breach of terms/│   │ Consideration given   │
│ conditions of contract   │   │ by both parties –   │
└────────────────────────────┘   ┌─────────────────────────────┐   │ supplier provides goods   │
                                     │ Sale must also comply with │◀····│ and customer pays for   │
                                     │ any relevant legislation   │   │ those goods   │
     ┌─────────────────┐   └─────────────────────────────┘   └───────────────────────────┘
     │ Legal situation │
     └─────────────────┘

┌────────────────────────────┐   ┌───┐
│ **Unfair Contract Terms Act │   │ **Sale of Goods Act 1979** – goods must comply with   │
│ 1977**   │   │ three implied terms   │
│ Not possible to reduce   │   └───┘
│ liability for any of the   │   │ 1. Title – seller has right o sell good   │
│ implied terms in the 1979   │   └───┘
│ Act   │   │ 2. Description – goods match any written/verbal description │
└────────────────────────────┘   └───┘
                                     │ 3. Quality and fitness for purpose – goods must be suitable │
                                     │ and fit for intended purpose   │
                                     └───┘

Normal remedies for breach of contract

- Customer agrees to pay in full.
- Customer returns goods and supplier cancels invoice.
- Customer retains goods but pays a reduced price.

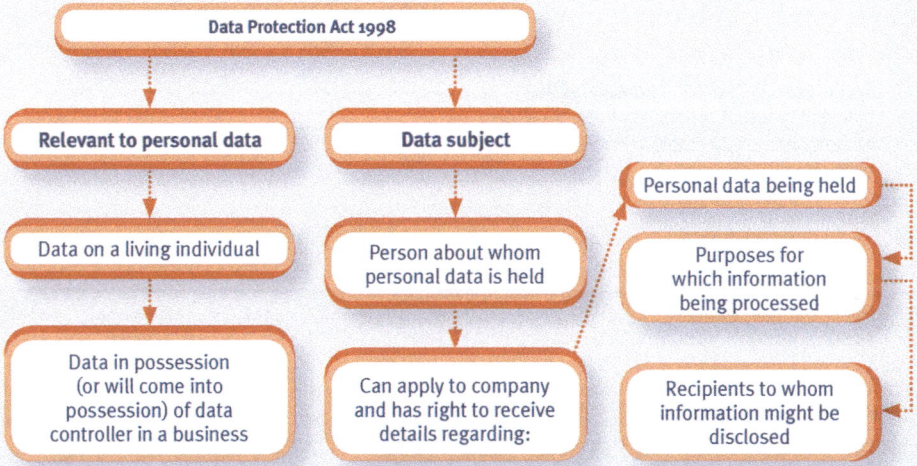

- Where individual applies for credit and is refused, company need not state reasons for refusal.

- However, name of credit reference agency must be given on request.

Exam focus

Try to ensure that you understand the different types of reports that can be used to verify the credit status of individuals and companies.

Debt collection

In this chapter

- Debt collection.
- Factoring debts.
- Finance factoring.
- Invoice discounting.
- Monitoring debt collection.
- Legal action.

Debt collection

Making debt collection efficient

- Send invoices out promptly.
- Ensure invoices sent to correct individual.
- Clear customer queries on invoice promptly.
- Send out statements where customers require.

Other efficiency factors

- Monitor credit limits – ensure not exceeded.
- Maintain good relationships with customers.
- Understand customer's system for processing invoices.
- Encourage payment by direct debit for standard amounts (e.g. rent).
- Encourage payment by BACS (Banks Automated Clearing System).

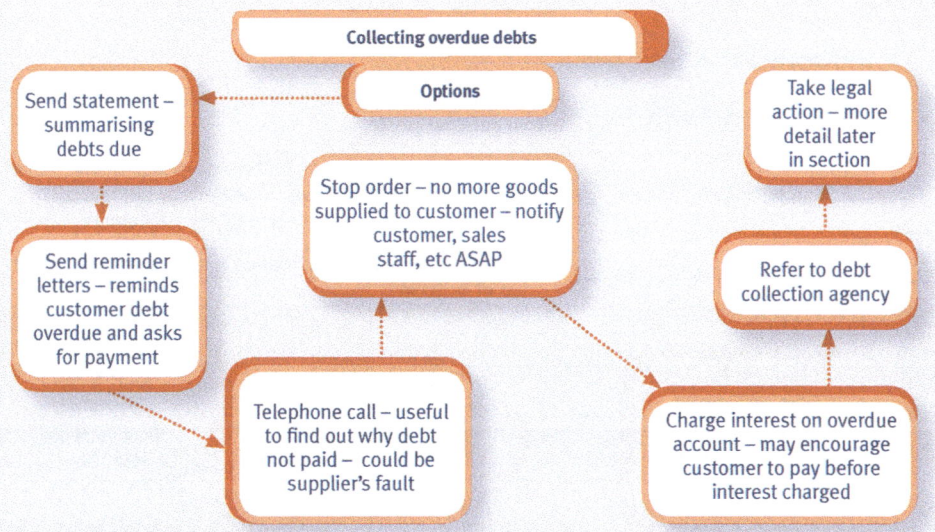

Collecting overdue debts

Options

Send statement – summarising debts due

Send reminder letters – reminds customer debt overdue and asks for payment

Telephone call – useful to find out why debt not paid – could be supplier's fault

Stop order – no more goods supplied to customer – notify customer, sales staff, etc ASAP

Charge interest on overdue account – may encourage customer to pay before interest charged

Refer to debt collection agency

Take legal action – more detail later in section

Other debt collection options

- Credit insurance – approved debts insured against non-payment.
- Debt factoring – authorising a specialist third party to collect debts (see below).

Factoring debts

Services available from a factor	
Receivables ledger administration	Recording of sales invoices through to obtaining payment from debtors.
Credit protection	Without recourse means factor bears any bad debts. With recourse means supplier bears cost of any bad debts; protection limited to credit checking new customers.
Providing finance	Factor provides short-term finance to a business, based on value of its unpaid invoices.

'Non-recourse'
Factor provides protection against irrecoverable debts

Factoring

'Recourse'
Client must bear loss of any irrecoverable debts

Finance factoring

Definition

Finance factoring: Factor makes cash advance to client as well as conducting receivables ledger administration and debt collection services.

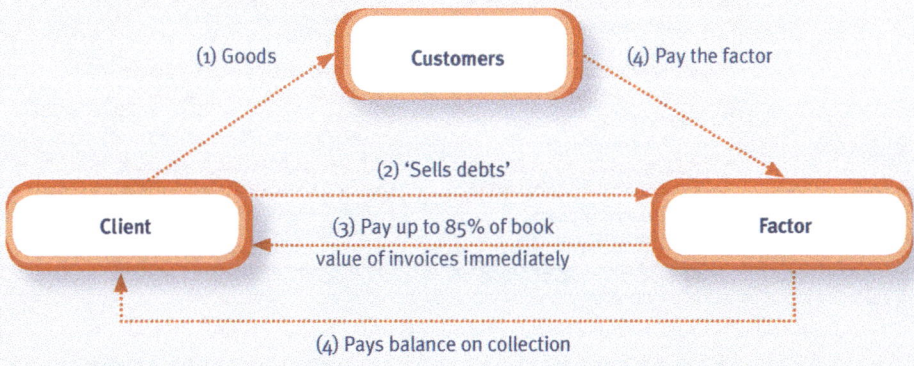

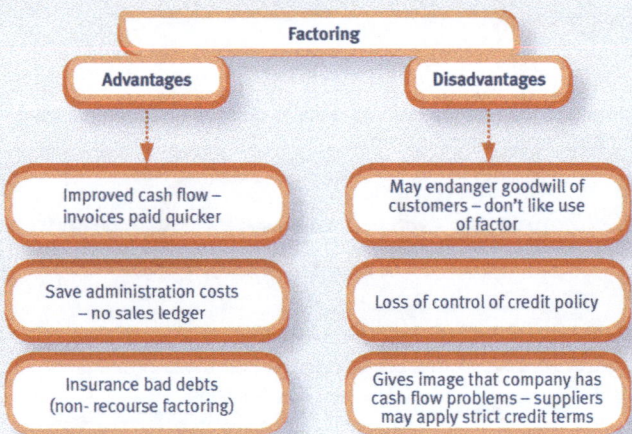

Factoring

Advantages

- Improved cash flow – invoices paid quicker
- Save administration costs – no sales ledger
- Insurance bad debts (non- recourse factoring)

Disadvantages

- May endanger goodwill of customers – don't like use of factor
- Loss of control of credit policy
- Gives image that company has cash flow problems – suppliers may apply strict credit terms

Choosing a factoring company

- Check whether non-recourse factoring is offered.
- Establish how overdue debts are chased (so as not to impact on goodwill of customers).
- Check basis of communication: factor > client – must be regular.
- Agree fee basis.
- Establish termination terms.

Invoice discounting

Invoice discounting: Raising finance against security of receivables without using sales ledger administration services of a factor. Organisations benefit from improved cash flows.

Procedure

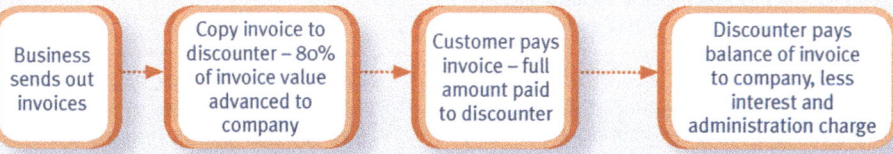

Business sends out invoices → Copy invoice to discounter – 80% of invoice value advanced to company → Customer pays invoice – full amount paid to discounter → Discounter pays balance of invoice to company, less interest and administration charge

Monitoring debt collection

Receivables monitored to:

- Ensure debt control procedures working
- Take measures against specific late payers.

Monitoring by ratios including days sales outstanding and aged debts analysis.

Aged debts analysis: Report showing total amount of debts owed to business, analysed between debts not yet due and debts overdue.

Days Sales Outstanding =

$$\frac{\text{Current receivables}}{\text{Sales for the year}} \times 365 \text{ days}$$

Note = current debtors NOT year end debtors

Key Point

An aged debts analysis (aged receivables list) gives organisations an indication of time taken by each customer to pay debts, and any potential irrecoverable debts.

Treatment of irrecoverable debts

```
                        ┌─────────────────────────┐
                        │  Bad and doubtful debts │
                        └─────────────────────────┘
                            ↙               ↘
```

Write off irrecoverable debts

- Debt unlikely to be collected
- Removed from sales ledger
- Debt written off to irrecoverable debt account

Set up allowance for others in debt

- Hope customer will still pay
- Debt remains in sales ledger
- Allowance made for debt
- Eventually customer either pays or debt is written off

Legal action

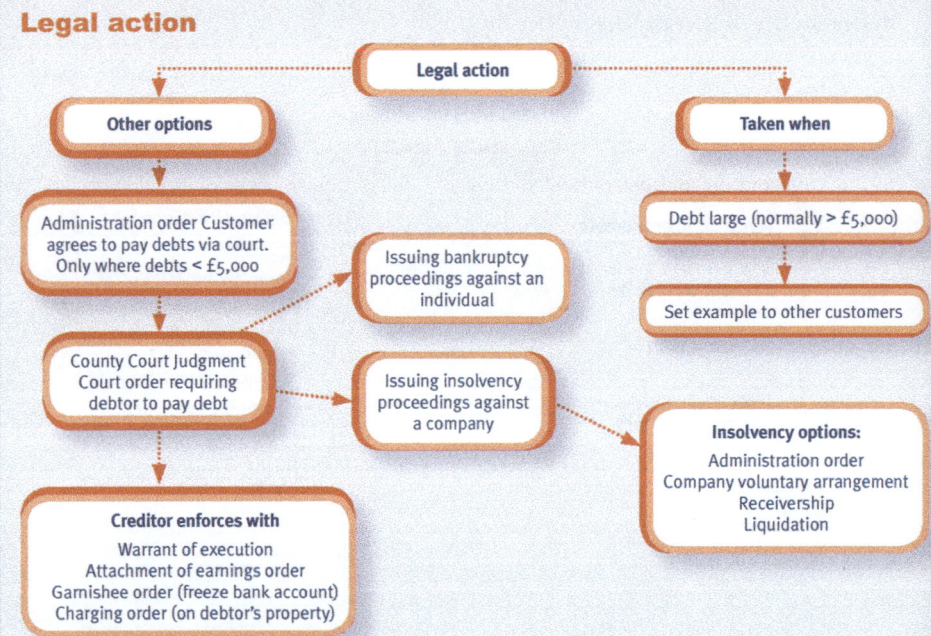

Legal action

Other options

Administration order Customer agrees to pay debts via court. Only where debts < £5,000

County Court Judgment Court order requiring debtor to pay debt

Issuing bankruptcy proceedings against an individual

Issuing insolvency proceedings against a company

Creditor enforces with

Warrant of execution
Attachment of earnings order
Garnishee order (freeze bank account)
Charging order (on debtor's property)

Taken when

Debt large (normally > £5,000)

Set example to other customers

Insolvency options:

Administration order
Company voluntary arrangement
Receivership
Liquidation

Insolvency options

Administration order

Specialist administrator appointed – company continues trading but all creditors involved in agreeing payment options.

Company voluntary arrangement

Agreement with creditors to pay part of balance (better than winding up and creditors receiving nothing).

Receivership

Company continues to trade, but

- Receiver appointed to take charge of specific asset and sell to pay payables, or
- Administrative receiver appointed to run entire company but also pay payables. If possible, control returned to managers after payables paid.

Liquidation

Company is dissolved. Decision by:

- Court (compulsory liquidation)
- Shareholders (voluntary liquidation).

Liquidator appointed to dissolve company and obtain best value for assets/pay payables.

If payable owed more than £750 (in UK), can apply for liquidation order.

Priorities for payment in a winding up

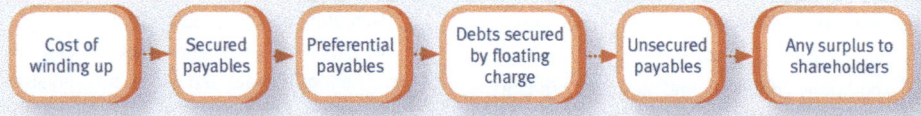

Debt collection involves many different options. Ensure you make reasonable decisions regarding collection in any exam answer; don't jump to winding up as a first option.

chapter

9

Financial management environment

In this chapter

- Structure of a banking system.
- Banks in the UK.
- The Central Bank.
- Financial markets.

Structure of a banking system

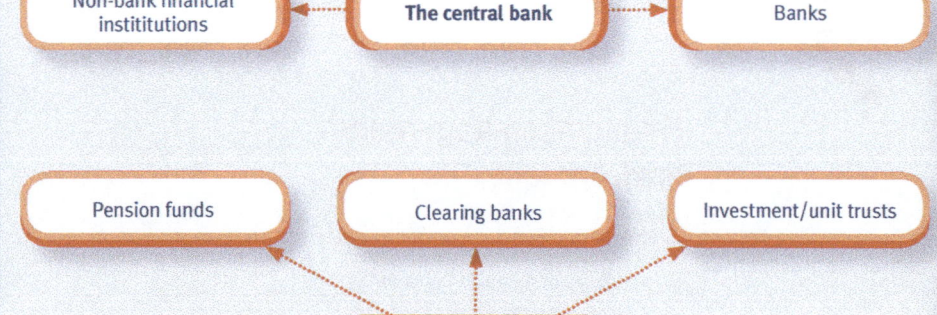

Definition

Intermediation: Refers to the process whereby potential borrowers and potential lenders are brought together by third party.

Role of financial intermediaries

- Expert advice.
- Expertise in channelling funds.
- Maturity transformation.
- Risk transformation.

Banks in the UK

- In the business of deposit lending and taking.
- Banks' liabilities = customers' deposits.
- Banks' assets = cash/operational balances, monies loaned and investments.

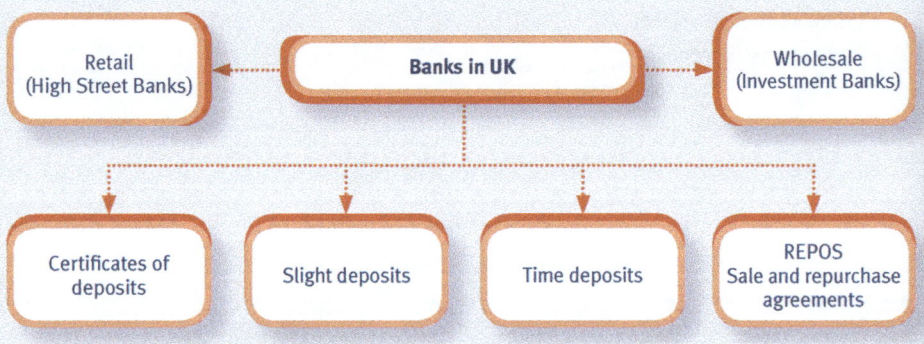

The Central Bank

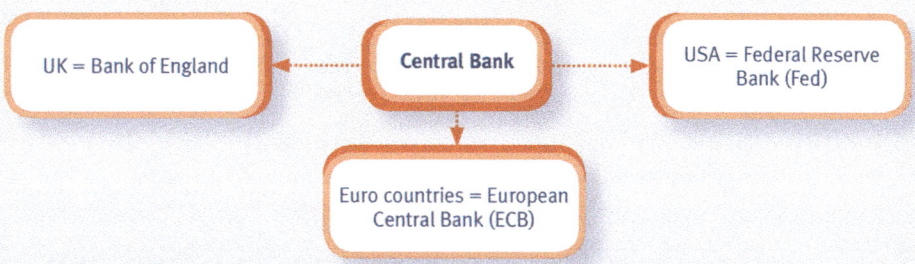

Functions of Bank of England

- Issues notes.
- Acts as banker to government.
- Manages government's borrowing programme.
- Advises on good banking practice.
- Provides liquidity to banks.
- Lender of the last resort.
- Operates government's monetary and exchange rate policy.

Financial markets

```
┌─────────────────────┐      ┌─────────────────────┐      ┌─────────────────────┐
│ Money markets       │      │ Derivatives market  │      │ Insurance market    │
│ Provide short-term  │      │ Provide instruments │      │ Facilitate          │
│ debt financing and  │      │ for management of   │      │ redistribution of   │
│ investment          │      │ financial risk      │      │ various risks       │
└─────────────────────┘      └─────────────────────┘      └─────────────────────┘

            ┌──────────────────────────────────────────┐
            │          Financial institutions          │
            └──────────────────────────────────────────┘

┌─────────────┐   ┌─────────────┐   ┌─────────────┐   ┌─────────────┐
│ Capital     │   │ Commodity   │   │ Futures     │   │ Foreign     │
│ markets     │   │ markets     │   │ markets     │   │ exchange    │
│             │   │             │   │             │   │ markets     │
│ Consist of: │   │ Markets     │   │ Provide     │   │             │
│ stock       │   │ where       │   │ forward     │   │ Exist       │
│ markets and │   │ primary     │   │ contracts   │   │ whenever    │
│ bond        │   │ products    │   │ to buy/     │   │ one         │
│ markets     │   │ exchanged   │   │ sell        │   │ currency    │
│             │   │             │   │ commodities │   │ traded for  │
│             │   │             │   │ at pre-     │   │ another     │
│             │   │             │   │ determined  │   │             │
│             │   │             │   │ price in    │   │             │
│             │   │             │   │ future      │   │             │
└─────────────┘   └─────────────┘   └─────────────┘   └─────────────┘
```

Primary financial markets:

- Provide meeting point for borrowers and lenders.
- Deal in new issues of loanable funds.
- Raise new finance for deficit funds.

Secondary financial markets:

- Allow surplus units to be sold to other investors.
- Help investors achieve:
  - Diversification.
  - Risk shifting.
  - Hedging.
  - Arbitrage.

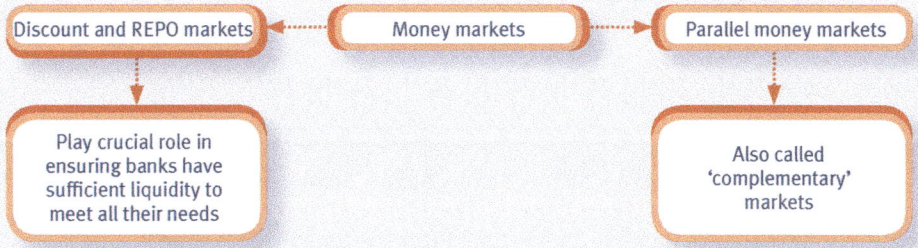

Discount and REPO markets ‹····› Money markets ‹····› Parallel money markets

Play crucial role in ensuring banks have sufficient liquidity to meet all their needs

Also called 'complementary' markets

Parallel money markets include:

- Building society market.
- Finance houses.
- Foreign currency market.
- CD market.
- Inter-companies deposit market.
- Local authority market.
- Inter-bank market.
- Commercial paper market.

10

The economic environment

In this chapter

- Money and monetary policy.
- Interest rates.
- Inflation.

Money and monetary policy

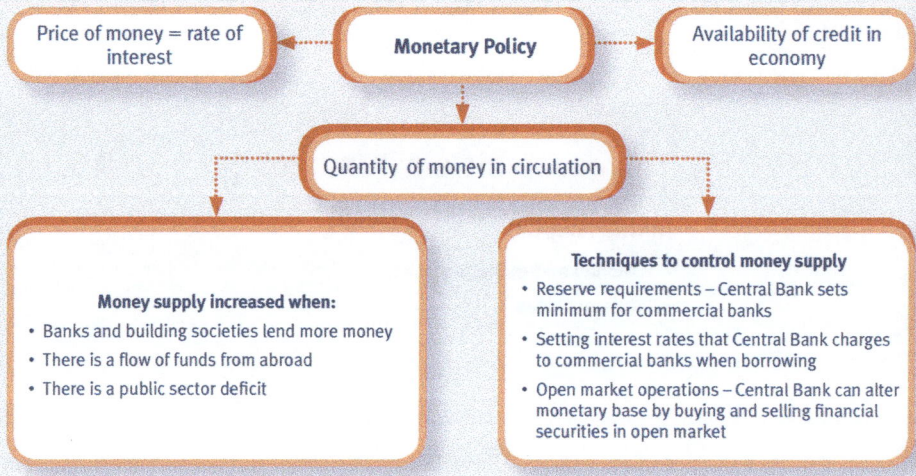

Monetary Policy

Price of money = rate of interest

Availability of credit in economy

Quantity of money in circulation

Money supply increased when:
- Banks and building societies lend more money
- There is a flow of funds from abroad
- There is a public sector deficit

Techniques to control money supply
- Reserve requirements – Central Bank sets minimum for commercial banks
- Setting interest rates that Central Bank charges to commercial banks when borrowing
- Open market operations – Central Bank can alter monetary base by buying and selling financial securities in open market

Key Point

Main instrument of monetary policy is short-term interest rates.

Interest rates

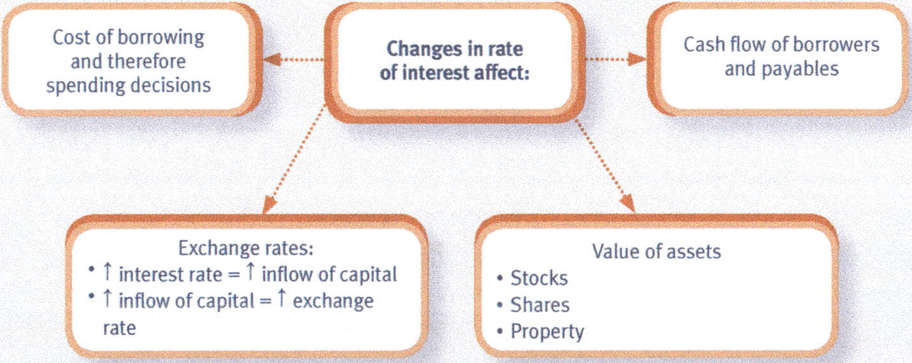

Cost of borrowing and therefore spending decisions

Changes in rate of interest affect:

Cash flow of borrowers and payables

Exchange rates:
- ↑ interest rate = ↑ inflow of capital
- ↑ inflow of capital = ↑ exchange rate

Value of assets
- Stocks
- Shares
- Property

Key Point

Changes in interest rates bring about changes in prices and inflation.

Interest rate = price of money

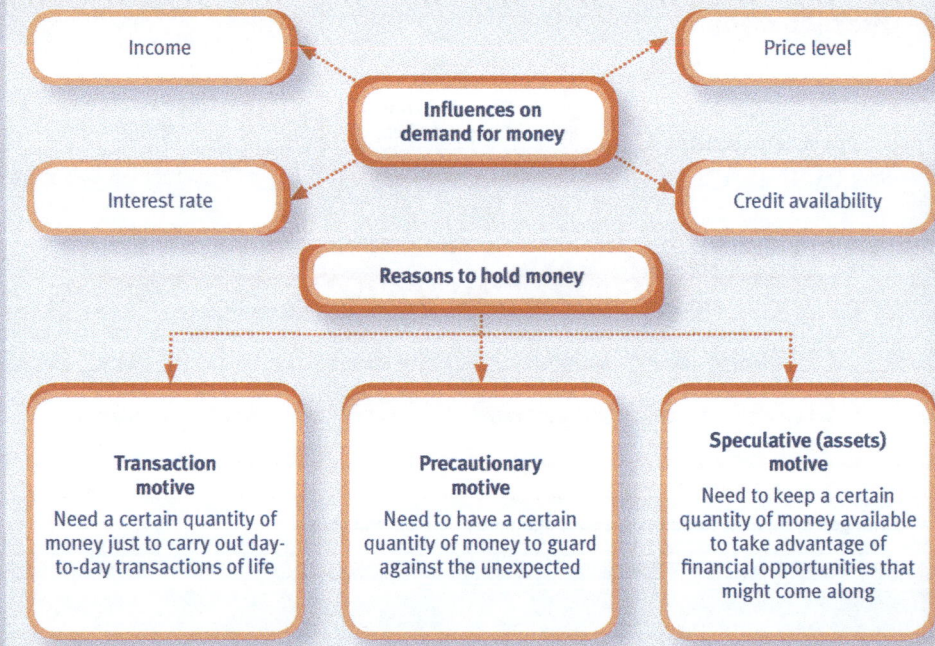

Types of interest rate:

- Fixed – rate stays fixed throughout life of debt.
- Variable – rate determined by reference to LIBOR or consumer price index.

Interest rate risk

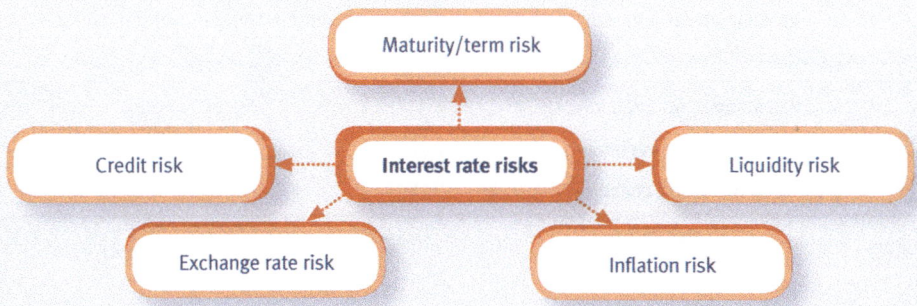

Nominal rates, real rates and inflation:

- Nominal rates reflect market yields.
- Real rates measure increase in real wealth.
- Relationship between nominal rates, real rates and inflation:

$(1 + N) = (1 + R) (1 + I)$

where:

N is the nominal rate of interest

R is the real rate of interest

I is the annual rate of inflation.

Inflation

Inflation: Rate of inflation measures the annual percentage increase in prices. Most usual measure of rate of inflation is RPI.

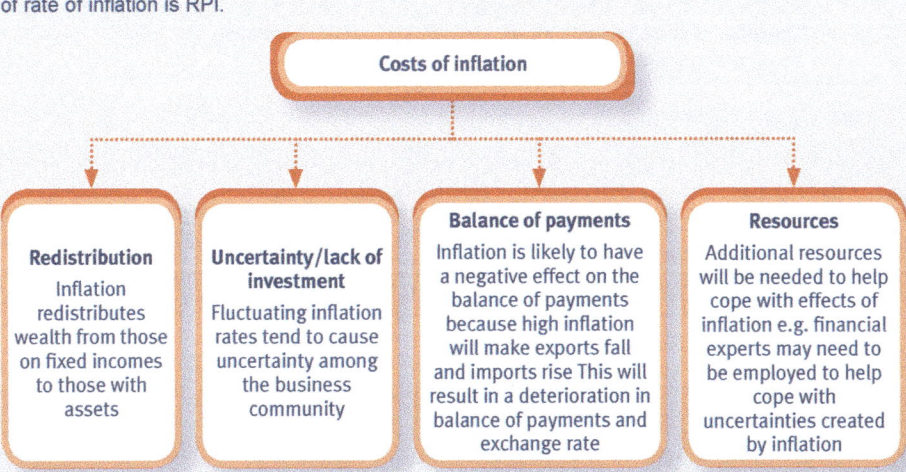

Costs of inflation

Redistribution
Inflation redistributes wealth from those on fixed incomes to those with assets

Uncertainty/lack of investment
Fluctuating inflation rates tend to cause uncertainty among the business community

Balance of payments
Inflation is likely to have a negative effect on the balance of payments because high inflation will make exports fall and imports rise This will result in a deterioration in balance of payments and exchange rate

Resources
Additional resources will be needed to help cope with effects of inflation e.g. financial experts may need to be employed to help cope with uncertainties created by inflation

Demand-pull inflation:

- Demand-pull inflation occurs when demand is high and suppliers, unable to meet demand, put up prices until the excess demand disappears.

- The situation can occur when consumers suddenly find themselves with more money in their pocket – such as after a tax cut.

Cost-push inflation:

- Cost-push inflation is caused by persistent increases in costs of production (e.g. wages increases).

- Companies react to these increased costs by putting up prices to maintain profit margins.

11

Short- and medium-term finance

In this chapter

- Short-, medium- and long-term finance.
- Raising short-term finance.
- Raising medium-term finance.
- Banks' criteria for lending.

Short-, medium- and long-term finance

- Major source of finance – accumulated earnings.
- New companies will not have access to accumulated earnings.
- Companies must make a choice between short-, medium- and long-term financing options.

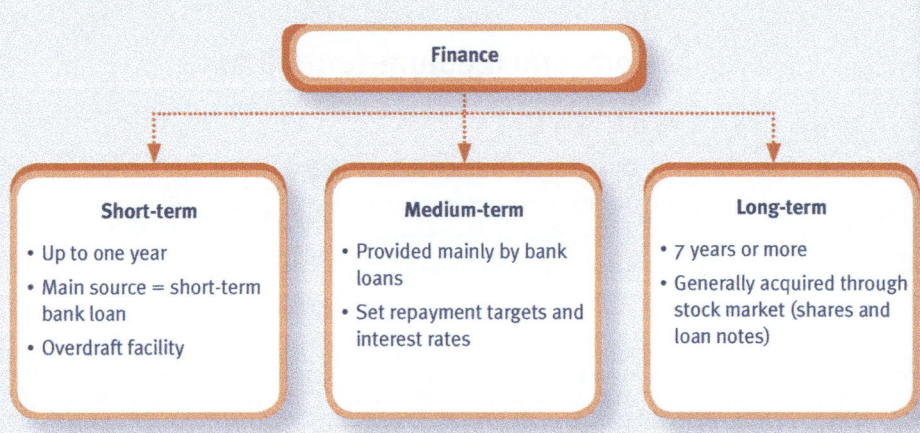

Finance

Short-term
- Up to one year
- Main source = short-term bank loan
- Overdraft facility

Medium-term
- Provided mainly by bank loans
- Set repayment targets and interest rates

Long-term
- 7 years or more
- Generally acquired through stock market (shares and loan notes)

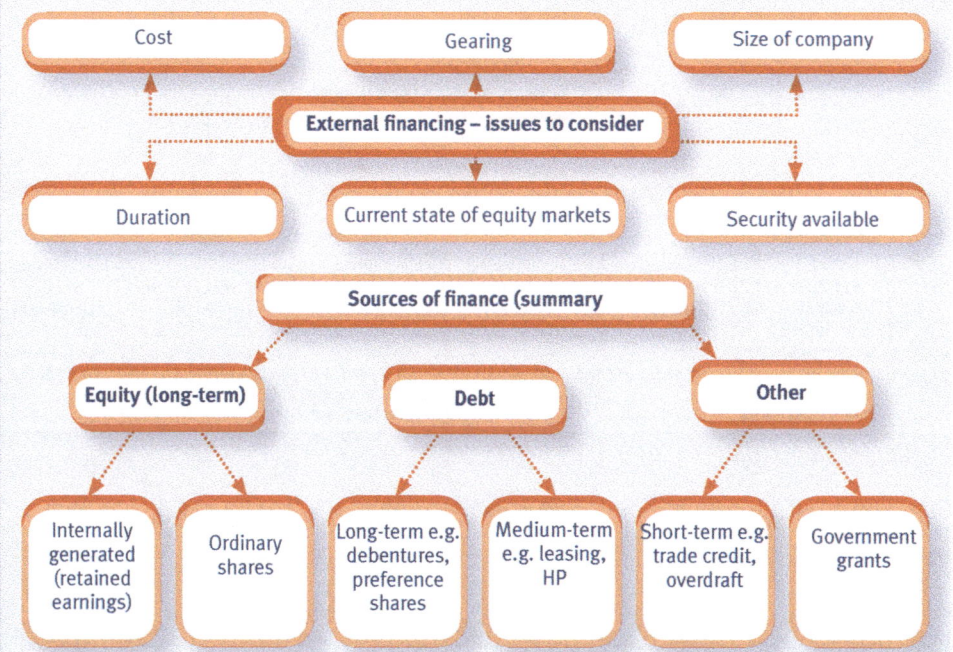

Raising short-term finance

Sources of short-term finance

Bank loans and overdraft	Trade credit	Factor finance	Bills of exchange	Acceptance credits	Commercial paper
Overdraft used to finance day-to-day expenditure. Loan finances long-term expenditure e.g. fixed assets	Allowing a customer time to pay for purchases	Improves cash flow but factor rate normally higher than loan interest	Short term when sold before maturity. Selling involves taking a 'discount' on the bill – receive less than face value	Bank accepts bills of exchange drawn by customer. Only available to large / trusted companies	Debt instrument issued on company by bank. Issued at a discount. On maturity, company pays full value to holder

Raising medium-term finance

Sources of medium-term finance

Bank loans	**Leasing**	**Hire purchase**	**Sale and leaseback**
Covered in earlier chapters	Provision of finance by specialist institution relating to purchase of capital asset. Lessor owns asset while lessee controls asset	Hire purchase company purchases asset – charges user interest on 'loan'. Asset only belongs to hirer when the payments are complete	Asset sold to third party, and then 'leased back' by vendor. Vendor continues to use asset but title with third party and lease payments made to third party

Banks' criteria for lending

C = Character
Background of individuals can indicate potential for success

A = Ability
Likelihood company can repay money

M= Means
Means and resources to run business and show bank as such

I = Interest/Insurance
Interest rate reflects view of risk/insurance cover to cover inability to pay

**CAMP ARI:
Banks' criteria for lending**

P = Purpose
Explain in detail why company wishes to borrow money

R = Repayment
Need to show bank company can afford repayments on amount borrowed

A = Amount
Establish correct amount that company needs to borrow

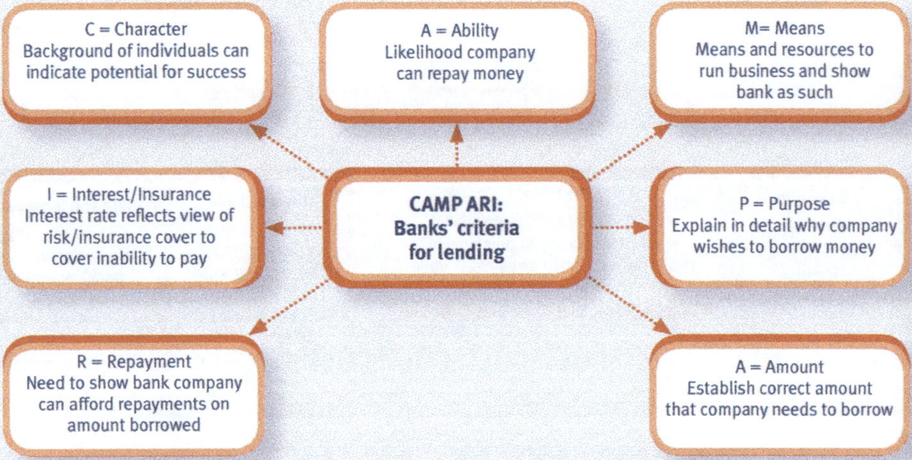

Exam focus

Ensure you understand the different ways in which a company can raise short- and medium-term funds and discuss which methods of finance are suitable for different companies.

12

Long-term finance

In this chapter

- Sources of finance.
- How a stock market operates.
- Equity finance.
- Choosing between sources of equity finance.
- Corporate bonds and loan notes.
- Hybrids of debt and equity.
- Summary of long-term finance.

Sources of finance

Long-term finance: Needed to finance long-term assets of company and some current assets. Should be suitable balance between long-term and short-term funding.

Debt or equity?

- Debt is regarded as cheaper source of finance than equity.
- Balance between debt and equity is partly a matter of judgement.
- Balance of funding must be considered if company wishes to increase long-term funding.

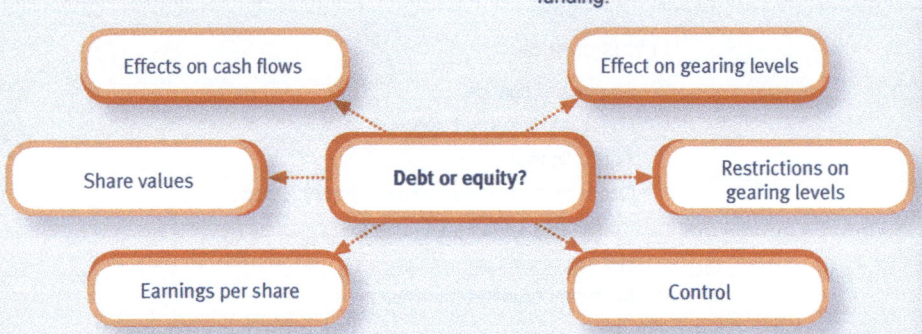

Effects on cash flows

Effect on gearing levels

Share values

Debt or equity?

Restrictions on gearing levels

Earnings per share

Control

Sources of long-term finance

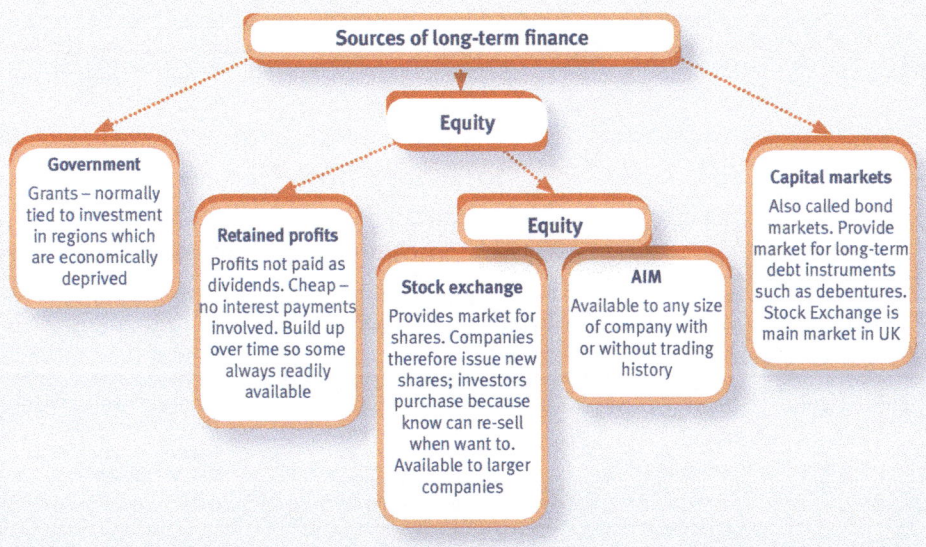

Sources of long-term finance

Equity

Government
Grants – normally tied to investment in regions which are economically deprived

Retained profits
Profits not paid as dividends. Cheap – no interest payments involved. Build up over time so some always readily available

Equity

Stock exchange
Provides market for shares. Companies therefore issue new shares; investors purchase because know can re-sell when want to. Available to larger companies

AIM
Available to any size of company with or without trading history

Capital markets
Also called bond markets. Provide market for long-term debt instruments such as debentures. Stock Exchange is main market in UK

How a stock market operates

Private companies list on the Stock Exchange to raise capital and provide a market in their shares

Stock

Official List
TOP TIER

- Market for large companies
- Trading volumes high
- Shares have high level of liquidity
- Shares offered to public
- Largest Official List companies – FTSE 100/250

AIM
SECOND TIER

- Junior market of London Stock Exchange
- Less demanding conditions than main market
- Too small for institutional funds to invest in
- Successful AIM companies graduate to main market

OFEX
THIRD TIER

- Not regulated by Stock Exchange
- Only requirement is that companies must produce accounts twice a year
- Trades only carried out on matched bargain basis
- Risky

Equity finance

Equity finance: The investment in a company by the ordinary shareholders, represented by the issued ordinary share capital plus reserves.

Sources of equity finance

Internally generated funds:

Comprise accumulated earnings plus non-cash charges against profit (e.g. depreciation) – can represent single most important source of finance for established companies

Rights issues:

Offer to existing shareholders to subscribe for more shares in proportion to their existing holdings

New external share issues:

- Private negotiation
- Placing
- Offer for sale
- Rights issue

Choosing between sources of equity finance

Equity finance:

- Not single source of finance.
- Group of alternative ways of raising funds:
  - Rights issues.
  - Placings.
  - Issues to general public.

Choosing between sources – consider:

- Accessibility of finance.
- Amount of finance.
- Costs of issue procedure.
- Pricing of the issue.
- Control.
- Taxation.
- Dividend policy.

Investor ratios: Used to indicate return likely from investment.

Ratio	Calculation	Use
Dividend per share	$\dfrac{\text{Total dividend}}{\text{Number of shares}}$	Shows income per share.
Dividend cover	$\dfrac{\text{Profit available to shareholders}}{\text{Total dividend}}$	Shows how many times dividend could be paid from profits.
Dividend yield	$\dfrac{\text{Dividend per share}}{\text{Current share price}}$ x 100	Shows dividend as percentage of share price.
Earnings per share	$\dfrac{\text{Profit available to shareholders}}{\text{Number of shares in issue}}$ x 100	Amount of profit that could, in theory, be paid to shareholders.
Price/earnings ratio	$\dfrac{\text{Current share price}}{\text{Earnings per share}}$	Current share price as a multiple of earnings per share – shows how many years dividends required to repay investment in share.

Key Point

Note higher gearing means EPS more volatile. Fall in profits means EPS falls faster in a highly geared company – interest repayments form larger part of before interest and tax – and must still be paid.

Corporate bonds and loan notes

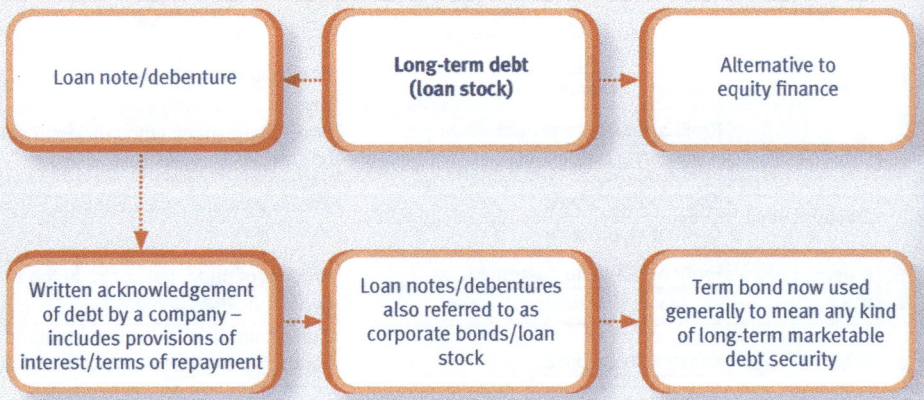

Loan note/debenture

Long-term debt
(loan stock)

Alternative to
equity finance

Written acknowledgement
of debt by a company –
includes provisions of
interest/terms of repayment

Loan notes/debentures
also referred to as
corporate bonds/loan
stock

Term bond now used
generally to mean any kind
of long-term marketable
debt security

Hybrids of debt and equity

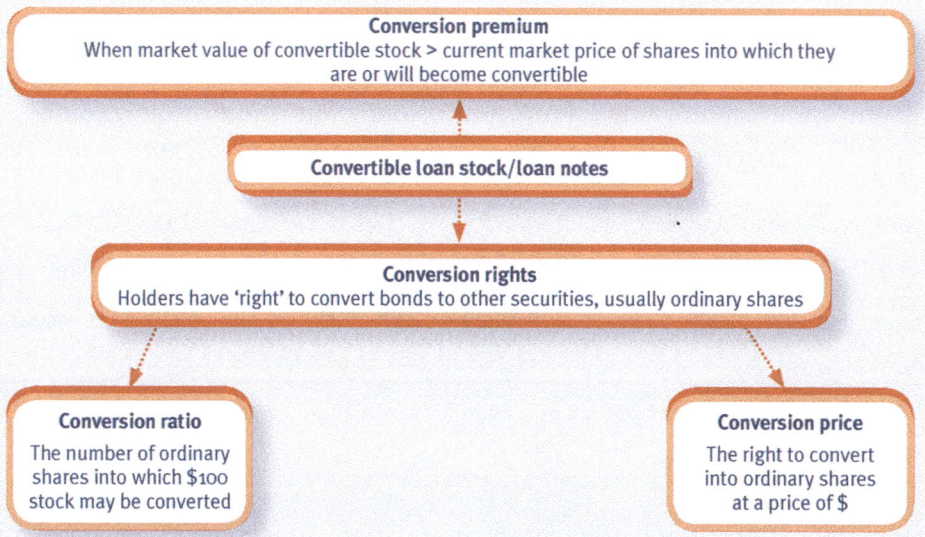

Conversion premium
When market value of convertible stock > current market price of shares into which they are or will become convertible

Convertible loan stock/loan notes

Conversion rights
Holders have 'right' to convert bonds to other securities, usually ordinary shares

Conversion ratio
The number of ordinary shares into which $100 stock may be converted

Conversion price
The right to convert into ordinary shares at a price of $

Key Point

Warrant: Gives holder 'right' to subscribe for a certain number of ordinary shares at a pre-determined price at a fixed date in the future.

Loan stock NOT converted into equity

Loan stock with warrants

Loan stock therefore continues until it is redeemed

Bond holders make cash payment to acquire shares and retain their loan stock

Summary of long-term finance

Type	Voting rights	Income	Security / amount on winding up
Ordinary shares	Vote in general meeting	Dividends when proposed by directors	Surplus funds after all other payables
Cumulative preferred shares	None	Fixed amount each year – payable in next year if missed in current year	Fixed amount per share after all other payables apart from ordinary shareholders
Non-cumulative preferred shares	None	Fixed amount per year but arrears do not accumulate	Fixed amount per share after all payables except those above
Secured loan notes	None	Fixed amount expressed as percentage of nominal amount	Fixed charge on specific assets
Unsecured loan notes	None	Fixed amount expressed as percentage of nominal amount	Floating charge on assets (normally receivables/ inventory)

Exam focus

Make sure you understand the factors to consider when deciding on how much equity and how much loan finance a business should have.

13

Sources of finance for small and medium-sized enterprises

In this chapter

- Small and medium-sized enterprises (SMEs).
- Problems of financing SMEs.
- Potential sources of financing for SMEs.

Small and medium-sized enterprises (SMEs)

Small enterprises

- < 50 employees
- Annual turnover ≤ €10 million (about £7 million or $14 million) OR
- Statement of financial position total of ≤ €10 million (about £7 million or $14 million).

Key Point

Wealthy individuals who once provided major sources of Venture Capital for SMEs are now persuaded by tax system to channel funds into large companies – this has led to problems with funding for SMEs.

Medium-sized enterprises

- 50 to 249 employees
- Annual turnover ≤ €50 million (about £34 million or $70 million) OR
- Statement of financial position total of ≤ €43 million (about £29 million or $58 million).

Problems of financing SMEs

SMEs need finance to grow and develop – however, most find it extremely difficult to obtain finance.

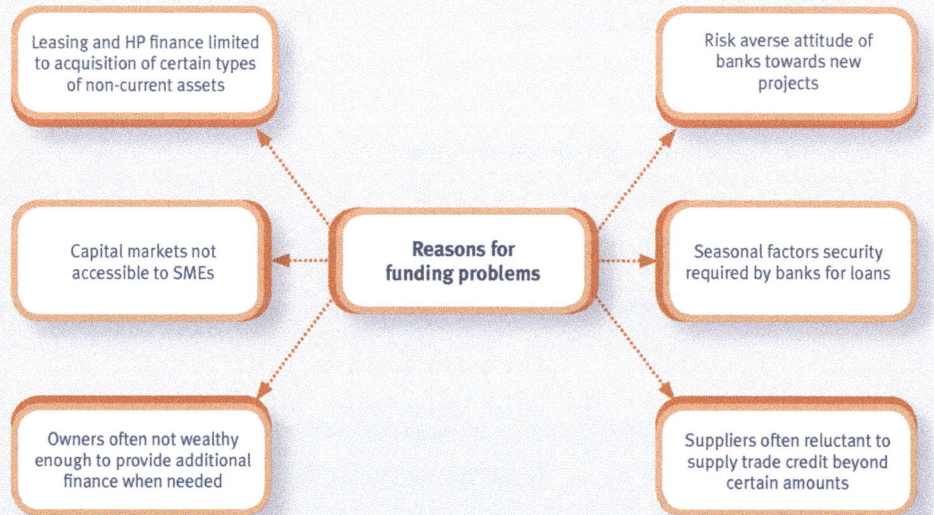

Leasing and HP finance limited to acquisition of certain types of non-current assets

Risk averse attitude of banks towards new projects

Capital markets not accessible to SMEs

Reasons for funding problems

Seasonal factors security required by banks for loans

Owners often not wealthy enough to provide additional finance when needed

Suppliers often reluctant to supply trade credit beyond certain amounts

Government aids for SMEs:

- Advisory services e.g. Business Links.
- Advice – Small Business Service (SBS).
- AIM – small firms market.
- CA 85 – Companies can purchase own shares.
- Tax incentives – Enterprise Investment Scheme (EIS).
- Loans – Small Firms Loan Guarantee Scheme.
- Finance.
- Tax concessions.
- Venture Capital Trusts (VCTs).
- Share Incentive Schemes.

Grants for research, development and innovation

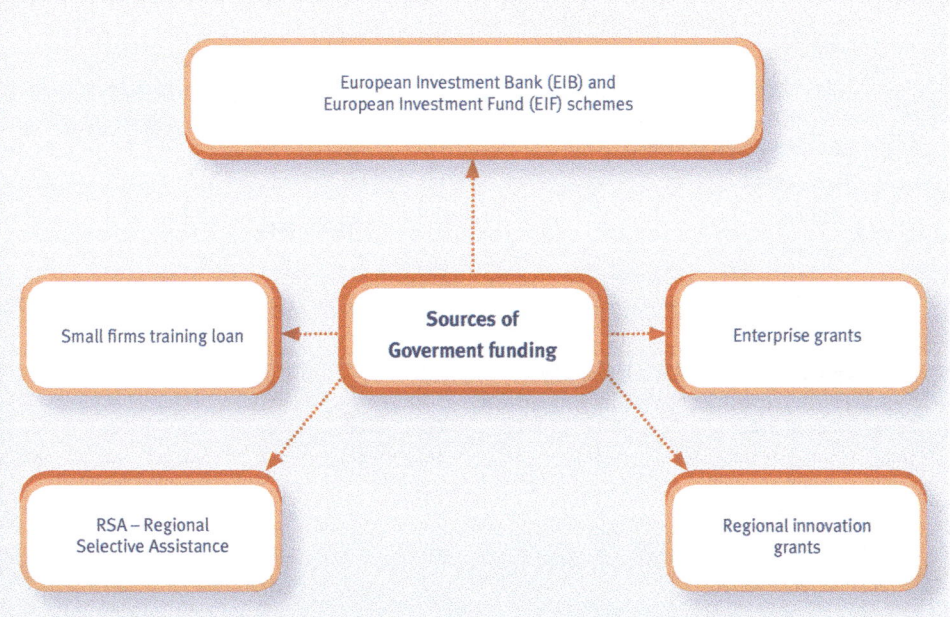

European Investment Bank (EIB) and
European Investment Fund (EIF) schemes

Small firms training loan

**Sources of
Goverment funding**

Enterprise grants

RSA – Regional
Selective Assistance

Regional innovation
grants

Potential sources of financing for SMEs

- Initial owner financing plus grants/ODs and loans.
- Business Angel financing.
- Trade credit.
- Leasing.
- Factoring.

- Venture Capital.
- Short- and medium- term bank loans.
- Mezzanine finance.
- Private placements.
- Public equity.
- Public debt.

Venture capital

Definition

Venture capital: Risk capital, typically provided by specialist financiers, both private and institutional.

Venture capitalists:

- Take large risk when invest in small company.
- Expect large return.
- Not long-term investors.
- Look for exit route to sell shares.

Venture capital funds/institutions:

- Largest in UK = 3i Group.
- Only invest if believe return will be high.
- Limit to funds available.
- Require basic information when assessing viability of new project (see diagram below).

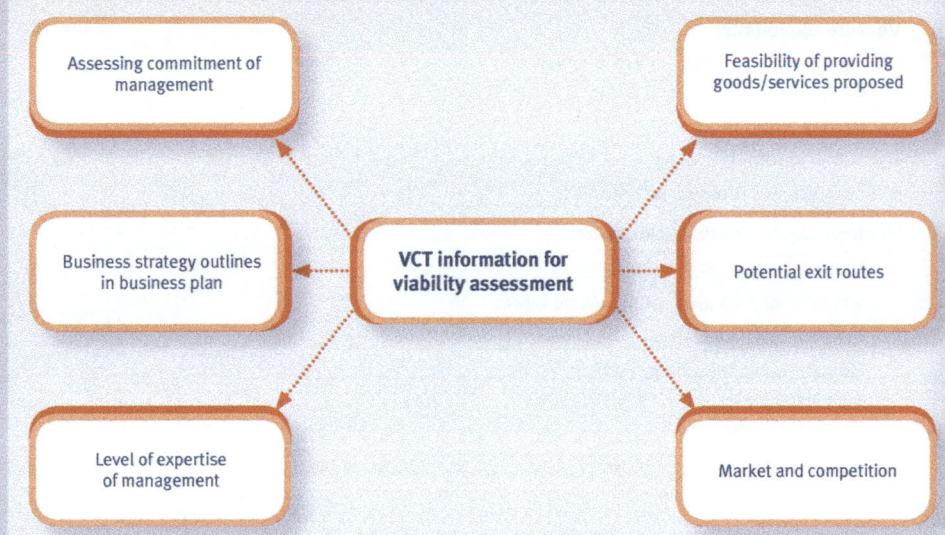

14

Capital investment planning and control

In this chapter

- Capital and revenue expenditure.
- Control over non-current assets.
- Capital budgeting.

Capital and revenue expenditure

Definition

Capital expenditure: Expenditure on productive assets which are used on continuing basis in activities of business.

Definition

Capital investment: Involves expenditure on non-current assets for use in project intended to provide a return (interest/dividends/capital appreciation).

Reasons for capital expenditure

Maintenance
Spending on non-current assets to replace worn-out assets or obsolete assets, or spending to improve existing assets

Profitability
Spending on non-current assets to improve profitability of existing business, save costs, improve quality etc

Expansion
Spending to expand business, make new products, invest in R&D etc

Indirect
Spending on non-current assets that doesn't have direct impact on profits of business

Revenue expenditure: Expenditure for the purpose of the trade, includes: salaries, services (telephone, rent, electricity etc).

Depreciation:

- Assets lose value over time.
- Loss of value shown as depreciation.
- Treated as revenue expenditure.
- Written off in statement of profit or loss.

Capital income:

- Arises when non-current (non-trading assets sold.
- Profit/(loss) included in statement of profit or loss.

Control over non-current assets

Authorisation:

- Management should authorise capital expenditure.
- Authorisation based on various criteria being met:
  - Payback period.
  - Rate of return achievable.
  - Degree of risk.
  - Effect on cash flows.
  - Comparability with competing projects.

Asset register:

- Details additions to non-current assets.
- Includes description, cost, expected life depreciation and NBV.
- Includes details of any disposals.
- Reconciled to general ledger.

Capital budgeting

Budget required to authorise, control and review capital expenditure.

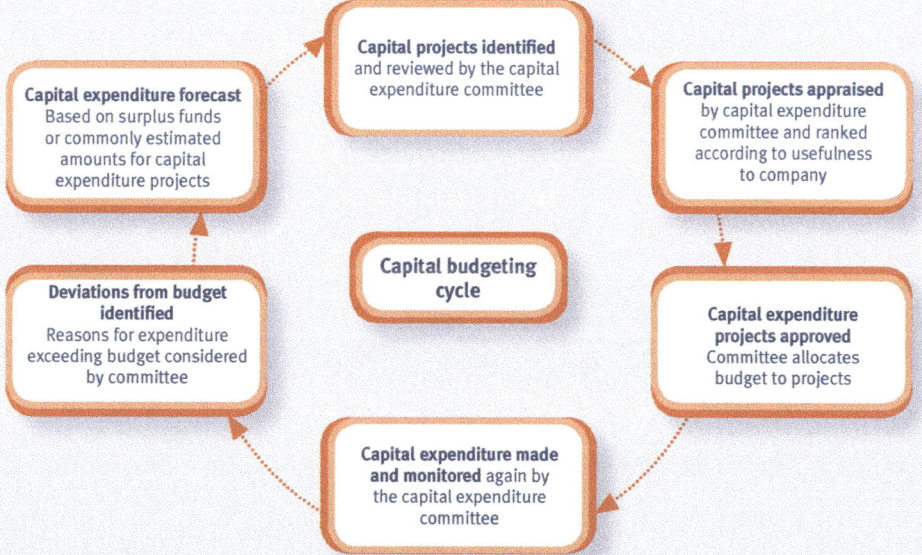

Capital projects identified and reviewed by the capital expenditure committee

Capital projects appraised by capital expenditure committee and ranked according to usefulness to company

Capital expenditure forecast Based on surplus funds or commonly estimated amounts for capital expenditure projects

Capital budgeting cycle

Capital expenditure projects approved Committee allocates budget to projects

Deviations from budget identified Reasons for expenditure exceeding budget considered by committee

Capital expenditure made and monitored again by the capital expenditure committee

Post-completion audit:

- Conducted by staff who are independent of original commissioning team.
- Determines the measure of success of a capital expenditure project.
- Draws management's attention to unsuccessful projects.

15

Capital investment appraisal

In this chapter

- Investment appraisal and cash flows.
- Accounting Rate of Return (ARR).
- Payback.
- Time value of money.
- Discounted cash flows (DCF).
- Net present value (NPV).
- Annuities and cumulative present values.
- Internal rate of return (IRR).
- Discounted payback.

Investment appraisal and cash flows

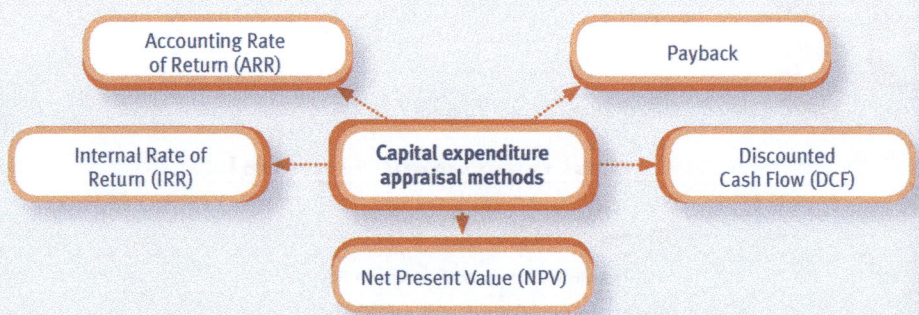

Accounting profits do not properly reflect investment returns – in capital investment appraisal it is more appropriate to evaluate future cash flows. The only cash flows that should be taken into consideration in capital investment appraisal are relevant cash flows.

Accounting Rate of Return (ARR)

Definition

Accounting Rate of Return: Also called ROCE. Expresses profits from project as percentage of capital cost.

$$ARR = \frac{\text{Average annual (post depreciation) profits}}{\text{Initial capital costs}} \times 100$$

Example

Initial cost of machine= $110,000

Depreciation of machine = $20,000 pa

Profit increase from machine $24,400 pa

$$ARR = \frac{24,400 - 20,000}{110,000} \times 100 = 4\%$$

ARR = 4%

Advantages – ARR

- Simple to understand and calculate.
- Widely used, expressed as %.
- Links with other accounting measures.

Disadvantages – ARR

- Ignores project life/timing of cash flows.
- Ignores cash flows entirely.

Payback

Definition

Amount of time expected for cash inflows from capital investment project to equal cash outflows.

$$\text{Payback} = \frac{\text{Initial payment}}{\text{Annual cash flow}}$$

Example

Initial cost of machine = $1,800,000

Annual cash inflows = $350,000

$$\text{Payback} = \frac{1,800,000}{350,000} = 5.1429 \text{ years}$$

or 5 years and 2 months

Payback calculations with uneven cash flows involve additional complications. See study text for comprehensive examples.

Advantages – Payback

- Simple to understand and calculate.
- Widely used.
- Minimises risk by giving greater weight to earlier cash flows.

Disadvantages – Payback

- Cash flows after payback period are ignored.
- Time value of money is ignored.
- Ignores overall profitability of project.

Time value of money

Time value of money

Invest money to earn interest or profits

Better to have \$1 now than
in one year's time

\$1 now can be invested for a year
to earn a return

Remember ! Now = time 0

DCF method takes into account time
value of money

Discounted Cash Flow (DCF)

Definition

Discounted cash flow (DCF): Investment appraisal technique that takes into account the time value of money.

DCF
=
Cash flow in year X
x
Discount factor based on cost of capital
=
Discounted cash flow 'now'

Example

Amount due in three years' time = $133,100

Cost of capital = 10%

Discount factor (from tables) = 0.751

DCF = 133,100 x 0.751 = 100,000

Procedure for DCF calculation:

1   Obtain all cash flows.

2   Obtain cost of capital.

3   Multiply all cash flows by relevant discount factor (as above).

4   Assume cash outflows occur at beginning of year (year 0 for initial expenditure).

5   Assume cash inflows occur at end of year.

6   Add results to show total discounted flows for project.

Cost of capital:

- Cost of funds for a business.
- Minimum return that business should make from its own investments.
- Expressed as a percentage interest rate.
- Assumed to be known figure for DCF calculations.

Net Present Value (NPV)

Definition

Net present value (NPV) method: Method of DCF analysis to calculate a net present value for a proposed investment project.

NPV method:

- NPV method discounts all cash inflows and outflows at company's cost of capital.
- Resulting present values are added up to give net present value (NPV).
- Result indicates whether to accept or reject project.

NPV > zero	NPV = zero	NPV < zero
Return from cash flows > cost of capital therefore accept project	Return from cash flows = cost of capital therefore project could be undertaken	Return from cash flows < cost of capital therefore project not accepted

Advantages – NPV

- Shareholder wealth maximised.
- Takes into account the time value of money.
- Based on cash flows which are less subjective than profits.

Disadvantages – NPV

- Can be difficult to identify appropriate disount rate.
- Managers may be unfamiliar with concept of NPV.
- Cash flows assumed to occur at year end – unlikely in practice.

Annuities and cumulative present values

Definition

Annuity: Fixed periodic payment which continues for specified time/until occurrence of specified event.

Perpetuity: A periodic payment continuing for a limitless period.

Example

Lease payment of $300 made for 5 years at 4% pa
Use annuity tables to obtain annuity factor = 4.452
Current value of payments = $300 × 4.452 = $1,336

Based on future cash flows, but 'discounts' these to show their present or current value.
Present value = amount to invest now at cost of capital to receive specific cash flow at some future date.

Internal Rate of Return (IRR)

Definition

Internal rate of return method (IRR): Annual percentage return achieved by a project where sum of discounted cash inflows = sum of discounted cash outflows.

$$IRR = i_1 + [\frac{NPV_1}{NPV_1 - NPV_2} \times (i_2 - i_1)]$$

where

i_1 = discount rate 1

i_2 = discount rate 2

NPV_1 is NPV at discount rate of i_1, and

NPV_2 is NPV at discount rate of i_2

Procedure for IRR calculation:

1 Calculate NPV for a project using two different discount rates.

2 Discount rates chosen to try to obtain one positive and one negative NPV. (**Note**: ignore minus sign on negative NPV.)

3 Enter results into formula above.

4 Calculate IRR.

Example

NPV1 = $3,440 at 15%

NPV2 = -$1,256 at 20%

$$15\% + [\frac{3,440}{3,440 + 1,256} \times 20\% - 15\%)]$$

$$= 15\% + 3.7\% = 18.7\%$$

Advantages – IRR

- Results expressed as simple % – easy to understand.
- Takes into account the time value of money.
- Indicates sensitivity of decisions to change in interest rates.

Disadvantages – IRR

- Can be confused with ARR or ROCE because expressed as %.
- May give conflicting recommmendations to NPV.
- Cannot accommodate changes in interest rates over life of project.

KAPLAN PUBLISHIN

Discounted payback

Discounted payback: Similar to simple payback method but cash flows disounted at company's cost of capital.

Discounted payback is determined by calculating cumulative NPV each year as shown below.

Year	Cash low	Discount factor at 10%	Present value	Cumulative NPV
	$		$	$
0	(75,000)	1.000	(75,000)	(75,000)
1	25,000	0.909	22,725	(52,275)
2	30,000	0.826	24,780	(27,495)
3	24,000	0.751	18,024	(9,471)
4	18,000	0.683	12,294	2,823
5	10,000	0.621	6,210	9,033
			+ 9,033	

Advantages – Disounted payback

- Easy to calculate and understand.
- Ensures project has positive NPV (not the case with simple payback).
- Reject projects taking long time to obtain positive NPV – future cash flows uncertain.

Disadvantages – Discounted payback

- Choice of payback period is arbitrary.
- Ignores size of NPV (projects with earlier payback selected – although longer payback projects may have larger NPV).

Exam focus

There are lots of calculations to be comfortable with in this section. Practise them by looking at lots of past exam questions.

Index